BEYOND
Xs and Os

Merry Christmas!

Wayne Jr 2016

BEYOND Xs AND Os

WHAT I LEARNED ABOUT FRIENDSHIP
AND SUCCESS FROM A COLLEGE FOOTBALL LEGEND

THOMAS J. BERTHEL
AND
HAYDEN FRY

Skyhorse Publishing

Skyhorse Publishing books may be purchased in bulk at
special discounts for sales promotion, corporate gifts, fund-
raising, or educational purposes. Special editions can also be
created to specifications. For details, contact the Special Sales
Department, Skyhorse Publishing,
555 Eighth Avenue, Suite 903, New York, NY 10018 or
info@skyhorsepublishing.com.

www.skyhorsepublishing.com

10 9 8 7 6 5 4 3 2 1

Library of Congress Cataloging-in-Publication Data

Berthel, Thomas J.
Beyond Xs and Os : what I learned about friendship and
success from a college football legend / Thomas J. Berthel and
Hayden Fry.
p. cm.
Includes bibliographical references and index.
ISBN 978-1-61608-113-3 (hardcover : alk. paper)
1. Fry, Hayden, 1929- 2. Football coaches--United States. 3.
Football--Coaching--Philosophy. 4. Character. 5. Success. I.
Fry, Hayden, 1929- II. Title.
GV939.F77B47 2010
796.332092--dc22
[B]
                                        2010021102
Printed in the United States of America

TO MY WIFE Deanna, my daughter Paige, and my son Brandon—their inspiration in good times and bad over the years has always motivated me to be better.

—Tom Berthel

CONTENTS

FOREWORD

SO MANY PEOPLE have celebrated, and continue to celebrate, the story of Coach Fry and the Iowa Hawkeyes. Fewer people know the story of Tom Berthel and how he built a multimillion-dollar company from the ground up. And even fewer know the great story of the friendship that these two men share. The following chapters provide a snapshot of their relationship and challenge all of us to really think about what it takes to achieve and maintain success.

Even though Tom is a business executive and I am a football coach, we both owe a great deal of our success to the mentoring of Coach Fry. In fact, most of what I have learned about college coaching started with his direction and guidance. Whether it was how a program should be run, how to mentor others, how to hire people, or how to recruit, the foundation of my own story was built upon what I learned during my early coaching years at Iowa.

By the time Coach Fry hired me, he and his staff had been in the building process for two years, and a lot of the heavy lifting had already been done. They had experienced several close games and tough losses, and the team was very, very tired of losing. What impressed me was that everybody had their minds solidly set on achieving a winning season, even though it hadn't happened yet. Coach Fry and his staff had certainly been successful at instilling an attitude of winning.

During the year prior to my arrival at Iowa, I was a graduate assistant at the University of Pittsburgh, where we finished second in the nation and were blessed with a team of very talented players. In fact, eleven of our seniors were drafted that year, and three of them were first-round picks.

We didn't have that sort of talent at Iowa in the early eighties. Ron Hallstrom went in the first round and Andre Tippett in the second of the 1982 draft, but the majority of our players were free-agent, good college types rather than NFL prospects. Still, what Coach Fry lacked in team talent, he made up for in a demanding work schedule, and by instilling a true sense of team in everybody. It was steep and fast-paced, but it was all good because we were unified for a single purpose. Coach Fry set the bar high and it paid off. Not only did we achieve a winning season, but we also earned a Big Ten Championship and an invitation to the Rose Bowl. It was an amazing story.

Needless to say, I've spent a lot of time thinking about what happened at Iowa in the 1980s, reflecting on methods and strategies. First, there was the staff. I don't think there was a guy on staff that was not an underdog in terms of having an opportunity to coach at the University of Iowa. Nobody but Coach Fry would have even given me an interview, let alone hired me. I was young and had limited experience, but for whatever reason, he invited me out and then asked me to join the staff. I learned a very valuable lesson from that. Even though everybody had a public opinion about what he should do and who he needed to hire, he did what he felt was right and stood behind it. That took an unbelievable amount of courage.

In addition to hiring me, Coach Fry brought in Barry Alvarez, a successful high school coach in Mason City, and Bill Brashier, who was on the staff that had been fired at North Texas prior to Coach Fry going there. Bill Snyder and Carl Jackson joined Hayden at North

Texas and then moved with him to Iowa. Both coached high school football for many years, and Bill also worked as an offensive coordinator at Austin College, a Division III school, prior to joining Hayden's staff at North Texas. The point is that there were certainly guys with more impressive résumés, but Coach Fry saw something in each of us that he believed in; he was not always about hiring or recruiting the most acclaimed or highly decorated people. He obviously wanted people with some level of expertise, but most important, he wanted good people who were team players. In football, that's everything. We were all on the same page, and that is one of the things I enjoyed so much about being on that staff. We just had a great camaraderie, and there's no doubt in my mind that it was not by accident. Coach Fry selected people who were going to mesh well together, coaches and players alike.

Once he had the "right people," he was deliberate in building a culture that allowed us to get out of our own way and succeed. Typically, coaches and competitors want to keep one foot on the gas, continually pushing harder, but Coach Fry has an amazing way of knowing when less is more. I can remember being in the locker room prior to the 1984 Freedom Bowl, preparing to play Texas. I think he sensed that all of us were pretty tight, and we all knew how much a win would mean to him, since he was from Texas. After giving the team a little talk before the game, Coach finished off with a god-awful joke about Texas belt buckles and the room busted up laughing. It was totally out of left field and completely relaxed everybody in the room. The rest is history. We went out and played a tremendous football game, winning 55–17.

Another memory of Coach Fry's ability to get the team refocused for crucial games came prior to a midseason game in 1987. We were 4–3 and struggling to gain momentum. It seemed to be one step forward, one step back, and he obviously knew that a good belly laugh could be the fuel we all needed to get in sync. Before Coach Fry came into the locker room, one of our players got up in front of the team with a cardboard cutout of Coach's face. He got really animated, gesturing and talking like Coach Fry. . . . Of course, the whole team was laughing. In the midst of it all, Coach came into the room, behind the player, and started miming that he was strangling the guy. Well, the laughter got louder and the player kept going because he thought it was all about him. He had no idea that he'd just been busted. We ended up winning six straight games after that, and I've often wondered if the whole thing was orchestrated. It was just too coincidental. Coach Fry was a master at knowing when to do things like that. It is a gift.

I don't think any of us knew at the time how demanding it was to be the head coach of a college program. Coach Fry made it look so easy and seemed to take everything in stride. I will never forget calling him a couple weeks after accepting my first head coaching job at the University of Maine. As soon as he answered I said, "Coach, how in the world did you ever do it, and how did you make it look so effortless?" He just chuckled, like a dad would do. I guess I always thought he was drinking coffee and reading the paper behind those closed office doors; I found out in a hurry that there's a lot more to it than that.

All of us who worked for Coach Fry picked up many of his values, ideas, and even his traits. As Tom explains in the following pages, Coach is one of a kind, and I would certainly never attempt to duplicate him or pretend to have his charisma or charm. One thing I learned a long time ago is that you cannot be somebody you're not. That's why they call it mentoring, and not cloning. I'm fortunate to have had more than one mentor in my lifetime: my father, Coach Fry, and Joe Moore, my high school coach and former boss at Pittsburgh. The personalities of all three men are very different than mine, and I've had to figure out how to learn from them while being true to myself and doing things that fit my own personality. Obviously, that is what Tom has been doing for years—listening and observing Coach Fry, and then making it his own.

Most of us are successful in life because somewhere along the way somebody took a special interest in us. Needless to say, I am so appreciative and have always felt indebted to Coach Fry for taking a risk on me. He gave me a solid start, personally and professionally, and I feel very fortunate that our current coaching staff at Iowa is much like that of Coach Fry's staff in the 1980s.

My deepest thanks to Tom Berthel, for sharing his own story in *Beyond Xs and Os*; in doing so, he is helping the rest of us to celebrate the life and contributions of Coach Fry. As you read, I invite you to enjoy some great football memories; to set a new goal or follow through on an old one; and, most important, to consider the people in your own life who may need someone to believe in them.

Enjoy . . . and Go Hawks!

—**Coach Kirk Ferentz**
University of Iowa

INTRODUCTION

DESPITE THINKING THAT we have laid out the best of plans, sometimes we go through life wondering where we are headed and what direction we should take. Working hard to succeed has always been foremost in my mind. Meeting Hayden Fry was a defining moment in my life, even though I wouldn't recognize it for some time. I assume that many of his players and coaches realize that his stories, advice, and caring attitude helped shape them into better people. Slowly, and with specific intentions, he always works to bring out the best in each of us. From the locker room to the boardroom, he has woven together the magic of team, family, and the spirit it takes to succeed.

In this book you will learn about some of those ideas and how they may help you go through life more fulfilled. Although I never got to take the field for him in football, I took the field with him in life, and we became great friends in the process. Never wanting to disappoint him, I set out on this adventure after realizing how much I have been

Beyond Xs and Os

inspired by Hayden. Here is your chance to learn more about the philosophies of a legend. I hope you enjoy my story and leave with some inspiration for your own journey through life.

—**Tom Berthel**
April 2010

BEYOND
Xs and Os

1

THEY TOLD US WE COULDN'T

Discovering the personal desire to win

IT'S SATURDAY, NOVEMBER 26, 1966, and Hayden Fry is in the heat of battle, up to his neck in controversy. The Texas sun shines cautiously on Southern Methodist University receiver Jerry LeVias as he takes the field at Texas Christian's Carter Stadium in Fort Worth. History is in the making. The first black scholarship football player ever to play in the Southwest Conference, LeVias must play two games today—one against the TCU Horned Frogs, and the other against the symptomatic hate and violence of racial integration. Stadium security is beefed up in response to an anonymous caller, who has threatened to harm LeVias if he sets foot on the TCU campus. Fort Worth police and FBI agents comb the stadium, looking for a potential sniper. Even the Boy Scouts, serving as ushers, have been prepped to help with surveillance.

Jerry LeVias, center, with some of his SMU teammates

Unaware of the pending threat, players from both teams carry out routine warm-ups as LeVias tries to block out the sound of angry fans telling him he doesn't belong. A tempest of tension is growing, and in the midst of it, in the proverbial eye of the storm, is the confident presence of SMU head coach, Hayden Fry. "Just concentrate on what you came here to do," Fry tells LeVias, "and ignore everything else."

Coach Fry recruited LeVias to SMU and believed in his potential despite the school leadership's opposition to a black player. The SMU alumni didn't want him, either, nor did the other teams in the Southwest Conference. Even some of his own teammates didn't want him. But Coach Fry didn't see color. He saw an outstanding student athlete with exceptional academic ability. He saw a young man who would benefit the SMU program—nothing more, nothing less. It is this attitude that makes Hayden such a great leader and mentor to me and to so many others.

Hayden has an amazing ability to look past obstacles and see untapped potential; to anticipate what someone has the ability to do, well in advance of their doing it. He is always on the hunt for the next great breakthrough, and oftentimes it is someone (or something) no one else noticed. Once he finds it, he pushes hard and expects the best. On the field or in the boardroom, Hayden loves to work his psychology, and even though he is demanding at times, his approach is incredibly inspirational and thought-provoking. Hayden simply brings out the best in people. Often against the odds, his advice leads to a way out and a way up.

This toughness and determination was surely bred through the adversity Hayden experienced during his childhood in Odessa,

Texas, during the 1930s and '40s. His father was a butcher and his mother worked at the local movie theater. She earned one dollar a night and went nineteen years without a raise. Growing up in Odessa, many of Hayden's friends were black, and he enjoyed spending time with them, using money earned from salvaging scrap metal and soda pop bottles to pay for an occasional bus ride and a movie. On those bus rides, Hayden saw his buddies mistreated. At school, he saw their athletic talents disregarded. "About my sophomore year of high school it dawned on me that something was very wrong," Hayden recalls, "and I made a commitment: If I ever got in the position to help my black friends, I was going to do it."

LeVias and his fellow black athletes, like Hayden's childhood friends, were told repeatedly they couldn't succeed because of the color of their skin or their impoverished backgrounds. When we

Cora Fry, Hayden's mother

come across folks who have been kicked around by life, the way to help them is not by giving them a handout, but by providing them with a pathway to success. We have to look for ways to give people the opportunity to succeed. It is something that needs to be fostered in our world. Everyone has the right to succeed, and everyone deserves to experience the satisfaction and joy of hard work.

Petersville, Iowa

When Coach Fry originally interviewed for the position of head football coach at SMU, he made it clear that he intended to offer a scholarship to a black student athlete. The president of the college at the time, along with a hiring committee of nineteen bishops from the Methodist church, responded decisively, telling him he couldn't. So, Coach Fry walked away from the coaching opportunity and returned to his job as offensive backfield coach at Arkansas. Just a few weeks later, the leadership at SMU had a change of heart and offered Coach Fry the position. He accepted.

Hayden and I have many things in common, not least of which is a childhood littered with skeptics. In high school, Hayden

5

fought through adversity to become the president of his student body. I completed my college degree after being told during high school that college was unnecessary, and that I should be content to work for the rest of my life at one of the factories in my hometown. There are plenty of good, hardworking people who chose that route, but it wasn't for me.

During our childhood, my siblings (eight brothers and four sisters) and I attended a one-room schoolhouse in Petersville, Iowa. The school's outhouse and the long walk to get there were a real treat during the harsh Iowa winters. (Luckily that only lasted two years for me.) My family lived in a house on the property of the Catholic Church in town, where my father mowed lawns and dug graves in exchange for rent.

Jerry and Verna Berthel with twelve of their thirteen kids

Eventually, we moved 6 miles northwest to the still-small town of Delmar, Iowa, where my family made up nearly 5 percent of the entire population. Even though the town was small, we no longer attended a one-room schoolhouse. Instead, we spent our days in a school that had shiny tile floors, indoor plumbing, multiple teachers, and classrooms divided by age. We were really moving up in the world.

While my father, who never finished high school, never seemed interested in having any sort of deep relationship with me, he did teach me the importance of hard

Tom's graduation from the University of Iowa, MBA

work and how to push myself in order to complete a project. At a very young age I can remember waking up at four o'clock in the morning to help my grandfather collect mail in several small towns and then deliver it to the central distribution center. Later, I worked for my father's electrical business, repairing televisions and rewiring buildings on local farms. In my spare time, I swept floors for the janitor of our school for meager wages.

Despite the work ethic I developed, I was told repeatedly by teachers, coaches, and my own father that I shouldn't dream too big. College was not a realistic option for me. Instead, I was told that I should be satisfied with settling down and spending

7

my life working in our town, just like my father had done. I'm sure they had no idea that their negative feedback was actually fueling a fire that had been growing within me throughout high school. I wanted desperately to get away. I didn't know how it would happen, but every time they told me I couldn't, it made me more determined to prove them wrong.

In addition to enduring the usual growing pains of adolescence, I was raised during the scary and turbulent Vietnam War era. Every time I watched the television coverage of battles and death tolls, I grew more nervously aware that I was in line for the draft. I was fortunate to never be drafted despite maintaining my eligibility and refusing deferments.

My educational dreams were realized—first in 1974, when I graduated from St. Ambrose University with a degree in music, and again in 1993, when I earned an MBA from the University of Iowa. When I crossed the stage to receive my college diploma, I imagine my face probably looked much like Hayden's did the day he watched Jerry LeVias and his Mustangs defeat TCU.

Over the course of a very successful career, Hayden took on three losing college football programs. He chose these programs because everything about them screamed, "You can't." The players and fans were used to getting their butts kicked every Saturday. They were used to being told, "You can't win," and, whether they knew it or not, they were hungry for someone to believe in them again. Coach Fry walked into their lives, got in their faces, and said, "Pick up the ball, get back on the field, and show the world you're winners." A losing attitude was never an option for a Hayden Fry-coached team. Hayden loves the psychology of motivating people in the face of "You can't."

This is precisely the reason why his friendship has so profoundly impacted my life, both personally and professionally. I am a survivor. Despite a rough relationship with my father and an environment that attempted to push me down, something in me—in all of us—wants to win. I had the desire and drive to achieve my dreams, but I was also hungry for someone to believe in me. More important, I needed someone who would look past my quirks and blunders to the potential within—to awaken my confidence and to help me develop a game plan. This is something everyone needs now and then, and it's something we often receive from spouses, family members, friends, and coworkers without even realizing it.

In 1985, Fred Fisher and I became pioneers in the independent broker/dealer industry when we formed what would eventually become the company I operate today, Berthel Fisher & Company. The business of investments can be volatile, and we have experienced our share of ups and downs along with the rest of the industry. In the wake of the tech-market crash of 2001 and the aftermath of 9/11, we experienced the

Fred Fisher and Tom Berthel of Berthel Fisher & Company

largest downturn in market history when many sectors were already starting to collapse. Closer to home, a division of our company that had been highly profitable suddenly began to lose millions of dollars. As the company's leader, it was a time of great turmoil for me.

The year 2001 was tumultuous even before the attacks on the World Trade Center. In the beginning of this market storm, Hayden invited me to California, to play with him in the Pro-Am Coaches golf tournament. One of the longtime participants was unable to attend, and Coach wanted me to fill in for him. I wondered whether I could really afford to leave at a time like this—and to play golf. But Hayden, in his wisdom, knew I needed a break, and suggested I step back and use the trip as an opportunity to look at my current situation from a fresh perspective. So, anxiety stirring within, I went.

It was a three-day tournament chock-full of Division I coaches, played the first day at Spyglass Hill at Pebble Beach, one of the toughest courses in the world. I'm a fairly good golfer, but the difficulty of the course—combined with the star quality of the participants—made me more than a bit nervous. To top it off, in usual fashion, Hayden had set the bar high by telling everyone that he had brought in a "ringer."

We arrived the night before the tournament, and I was trying hard to present a confident exterior as we previewed the club and the stakes. Each golfer in a foursome was allowed to use his handicap, and the two best scores from each hole would be added together to create a team score. In all, the tournament presented an opportunity to win using either gross or net scores. The scratch golfers went for the gross-score win, and everyone

Tom and Hayden playing at Pebble Beach, May 2001

else went for the net-score win. While we all joked that the tournament was "all in good fun," every one of us knew better. Every team came to win. Why not? These were highly competitive, Division I coaches. Of course they wanted to win.

Words cannot describe the childlike awe I felt as I rode in the cart from the clubhouse to our assigned hole for the shotgun start. We were assigned a personal caddy who rode next to me, and the morning fog was just beginning to lift as we came over the hill to our destination. I could hardly grasp the breathtaking view as I wondered how in the world I had gotten there, next to Hayden Fry, and how many people from my hometown of Delmar would have given anything to be there in my place.

Beyond Xs and Os

The moment of truth arrived and we prepared to tee off number six. Cut through majestic pines, it's a 446-yard par four with a dogleg right and a cluster of bunkers surrounding the green to the left and right. Beautiful. I only wish the view had been enough to stop my heart from pounding and my knees from shaking. Assigned the clean-up position, I approached the tee box after my teammates had each made their shots. They had all been fine—nothing great, no one in trouble—and I did everything in my power to look confident as I stood at address. Knowing that I almost always hit my three-wood straight, I decided to go with accuracy over distance. I wound up with a power swing, struck the ball, and saw it float slightly left, but not too far left (I thought). Looking for the ball . . . still looking . . . where was it? Everyone in our foursome was looking, when all at once we heard a loud "crack." The ball had struck a low-hanging branch, which sent the ball high into the air and back toward the tee box. It landed next to the cart of the team playing behind us and bounced into the creek next to the cart path. Perfect.

Everyone was stunned, not sure whether to cry or to laugh. My first shot at Pebble Beach as Coach Fry's ringer was a disaster. All I wanted to do was pack my bag and head back to Iowa, but I knew I had to hit a second shot. Coach knew it, too. He didn't make a joke or try to console me. Instead, he simply sauntered up beside me and said, "Hit 'er out there, Tom. You can do it." Then he chuckled as if he was remembering one of the times he had punted on third down. Quiet confidence oozed from his voice, and all of a sudden, I relaxed. I approached the ball for my second shot, starting the hole with a three. This time I sent the ball straight down the fairway and I ended up taking a six for a double bogey and a minor victory.

My next hole brought a birdie on a par five (which, as it turned out, was not my last birdie of the tournament), and, with my handicap, an eagle. Setting up for a long putt late in the round, Coach again eased the tension in his usual and subtle way: "Don't worry about that putt," he said. "You're a lot better than I am. You know, I'm the only man in captivity that can hook a putter."

Looking back now, I see that Coach was teaching me a valuable lesson that day. He was showing me that leaders never stop casting vision, especially when their team members are down and out. He knew that I was doubting myself, and said just enough to remind me that mistakes happen, but quitting isn't an option. Mostly, he taught me the power of instilling confidence and the will to overcome adversity. It would have been easy for me to dissolve into a pool of self-pity on that first day. Instead, we went on to win the tournament, beating heavily favored teams from across the country. My first-tee nerves and embarrassment were completely overshadowed by the walk to victory alongside Hayden to accept the tournament trophy, which is still sitting in my office next to a photo of our team.

The whole Pebble Beach experience, as Hayden suggested, did give me a fresh perspective on my business situation, and I returned to Iowa feeling much more prepared to tackle tough decisions. The fact was, our company could survive. In the midst of chaos, leaders see opportunity. Regardless of the losses we were experiencing due to the slumping economy, we would survive by making the right decisions and by committing ourselves every

Tom Berthel at Pebble Beach

day to winning. Our tee shot may have hit a low-hanging limb, but it was time to "hit 'er out there" again.

Great automobile innovator Henry Ford once famously said, "Whether you think you can, or that you can't, you are usually right." The key word there is *you*. Whether it was the SMU administration telling Hayden that he couldn't recruit a black football player, my father telling me I couldn't go to college, or hole number six telling me I was out of my league, the path to success is littered with cynics. I've found, without exception, that my dreams have never been achieved by listening to external opposition, but rather by listening to internal optimism. There will always be people and circumstances screaming "You can't," but we have to tune them out and listen, instead, to the voice of our own dreams.

Rarely is the red carpet rolled out for us, leading us on an easy path to success. Instead, we have to carry it with us in our hearts and minds. Hayden is a red-carpet friend, always believing in my ability to win, always overshadowing the cynics, and always ready to roll out the red carpet for my next big idea. Who is *your* Hayden? Are you surrounding yourself with friends and associates who believe in your potential and truly want the best for you? More important, are you that sort of friend to someone else? People are standing in line to squelch your dreams and point out your mistakes. But if you're going to succeed in life, you must surround yourself with positive people—not people who drip with empty praise, but people who are willing to get in your face every now and then and say, "Pick up the ball, get back on the field, and show the world that you are a winner."

POSTGAME WITH COACH FRY

They told us we couldn't

There are thousands of books out there today about mentoring, and I'm sure most of them are worth reading. Still, my background in psychology tells me that it's just not that complicated. People want to feel valued and they need to be reminded of their goals. That's it. If you can offer that to people and take a sincere interest in their lives, then you'll be an unintentional mentor of the winningest kind. It really is that simple.

In fact, until I had read the chapters in this book, I never realized the impact my words and actions have had on Tom. I'm amazed at the things he says he's learned from me over the years (and still remembers), even though I never consciously set out to teach him a thing. I just enjoy being with him and seeing him succeed.

In the interest of full disclosure, however, the reason I took Tom to Pebble Beach is because I like to win and he's a good golfer. Plain and simple. The problem is that he almost forgot he's a good golfer. We all forget sometimes, and that's what I love about coaching. When people get uptight and start to lose confidence, there is no greater satisfaction than pulling them back from the ledge, setting them on solid ground, and reminding them of their goals. Anyone can do it. All you have to do is sincerely care about people and remind them to stay motivated in the face of opposition, to listen to internal optimism. That's what red-carpet friends do.

As Tom mentioned, I experienced a fair amount of opposition when I was growing up in Odessa, Texas. When my family first moved there, we lived on the wrong side of the tracks. In fact, I was raised so far out in the country that I thought anyone with a "two-holer" outhouse was wealthy. Daddy was a butcher in the grocery market, and I helped him at the

Young Hayden Fry with a golf club

store by wringing chickens' necks and plucking feathers, restocking all of the canned goods and the fruits and vegetables, and throwing down new sawdust each night to prepare the floors for business the next day.

When I wasn't busy at the store, I caddied at the country club and quickly learned that golf is chock-full of life lessons (especially with a handicap like mine). One of my favorite memories of caddying came in 1940. I was eleven years old and the Odessa Country Club was hosting a big tournament. One of the players came over from Fort Worth, but his caddy got sick and was unable to make the trip, so they asked me to carry the guy's bag. We walked three rounds together, one round each day for three consecutive days. He was a real nice guy, and in three rounds of golf he never said a word to me, never asked me about the yardage or anything else. (Being as young as I was, I guess I didn't blame him. I didn't know anything anyway.) After the final round on the third day, he shook my hand, said "Thank you," and handed me a twenty-dollar bill. Twenty dollars . . . I couldn't believe it. In those days, we earned a dollar for carrying a bag eighteen holes, which was real good money. Turns out, the guy's name was Ben Hogan. I wrapped my fist around that money and went straight home to show Mom and Daddy (a little concerned they'd think I stole it). We hadn't seen many twenty-dollar bills.

I followed Mr. Hogan's career pretty closely after that, and have never forgotten the lesson he taught me that week:

If you don't have something important to say, keep your mouth shut.

A couple of years later, at age thirteen, I went to work for the city: I pulled weeds, whitewashed tree trunks, and took on other odd jobs to beautify the town. When I was fifteen, I obtained an underage work permit so that I could be a rough-neck, roustabout, and pipe liner in the oil fields during summer vacation. It was a hard life for those guys. Back in those days the equipment wasn't very good, and I saw friends get their fingers cut off and their hands broken. At night, I'd see the guys come out of one honky-tonk, a beer in each hand, and walk into another honky-tonk right next door. They'd work their tails off all day long in the oil fields, risking (and then nursing) injuries, and then spend half the night in honky-tonks just to get up the next morning and start all over again. I loved all those guys, but seeing their lifestyle really motivated me to go to college.

I played football during high school, but Mom and Daddy never knew it until my junior year. It was different in those days. Many parents never saw a high school sporting event because they were working so hard just to put food on the table. When the bus dropped us off after practice each day, I still had to walk quite a distance to get to our farm, so it was late by the time I got home. My parents never questioned where I'd been, though, because I made really good grades in school.

When we weren't playing football, my friends and I loved to box. None of us had any money and nobody owned a car, so we had to make our own fun. There'd be ten or twelve of us guys and we'd draw a circle on the ground in the dirt. Then, we'd take turns boxing each other to see who could stay in the circle the longest. It was "anything goes" and real tough. (We may have been ahead of our time.) I'm really proud to say that in fifty or sixty fights, I never lost. Of course, I was too smart to go to Fort Worth or any other regional tournaments. I stayed away from that.

My childhood and early teenage years collided with World War II, when the government was rationing just about everything: food, gas, clothing, and even farm equipment. Dad knew that folks had become quite accustomed to eating Spam, Treet, and all that good stuff, so occasionally he invited my whole football team over for a meat supper (remember, he was a butcher). It was such a luxury during that time, and I really appreciated him doing that for my buddies.

The bottom line—and what Tom talks about in this chapter—is that life is what you make it. My family was poor, but I never felt like we lacked anything. I was expected to work very hard, but through that hard work I learned so much about the satisfaction of a job well done. I feared for my life, and Jerry's life, during the SMU days (more about Levi later), but we did a lot to change life for black athletes in that part of the country.

Opposition is only a downer if that's how you choose to see it. On the flip side, it can provide a wonderful foundation for success. Looking back at the circumstances and people who have brought you to where you are today can be a wonderfully motivating thing. Success will come when you can see the obstacles and the "you can'ts" as tools that have shaped you into the person you've become. Embrace them and use them as a catalyst to get you where you want to be tomorrow. No excuses. In the process, you might just inspire somebody else to do the same.

2

LOOKING LIKE A WINNER

Inspiring belief

BELIEVING IN MY ability to succeed is one thing. Inspiring someone else to believe in themselves is something else entirely. I think I was born with a certain amount of stubbornness in my gut, and it has given me the gumption to believe in big dreams in spite of, and maybe because of, the skeptics I have encountered. Even so, my company could never be successful based on my belief alone any more than Hayden could have achieved such a winning football record without creating a team of like-minded believers.

I wake up every morning with the confidence that my company can win, and, as the leader, it is my responsibility to inspire that same attitude in every team member and every customer. Don't get me wrong: Everybody on our team *wants* to be successful. They all *want* to win, but sometimes they forget that we *can*

Tom Berthel speaking to BFC reps

win. Whether in the boardroom or on the football field, it is the leader's responsibility to demonstrate a winning attitude and build a winning image the right way.

During the football seasons of the 1970s, many of my Saturdays were spent in the parking lot of University of Iowa's Kinnick Stadium. Portable grills with white-hot coals and coolers with ice-cold beer provided the perfect start to a day of great food and great fun. I and the thousands that joined me loved Hawkeye football, but we weren't really there in hopes of a win. A victory was a nice surprise now and then, but our expectations were low. We expected to lose. We were used to it.

Without a doubt, this attitude made Hayden as crazy then as it does today. He became Iowa's head football coach in 1979, and brought with him an unyielding winning attitude. Hayden's arrival at Kinnick Stadium was preceded by a seventeen-year losing streak, and a losing attitude that penetrated every aspect of the game, on and off the field. Not only did he have to convince ninety-some players that they could win; he also had to convince the assistant coaches, the university's administration and faculty, the student body, the media, and the fans in the parking lot.

Hayden still admires Hawkeye fans for sticking with their team through those losing decades, but he was not the least bit amused by celebrations of close losses or moral victories. It was time to start acting like winners.

His first step in instilling a winning attitude came at a press conference soon after his arrival. With cameras and audio rolling, Hayden turned to Willard Boyd, president of the university, and asked, "Mr. President, are you committed to having a winning

Coach Fry

Photo Credit: Ted Roeder

Hawks Storming the field

football program at Iowa just as much as you are committed to winning at academics?" Even though Boyd may not have cared much about football before Hayden arrived, having his full support for the football program on public record was a crucial step in getting folks to sit up and take notice. Boyd answered "Yes."

Next, Hayden turned his attention to the players, assistant coaches, and fans. The Hawkeyes weren't winning yet. In fact, it wasn't until his third season at Iowa that the winning would officially begin. But, in Hayden's mind, the winning had already commenced, and he never passed up an opportunity to generate a vote of confidence. "Where I come from," he likes to say, "it's called selling the sizzle before the steak."

The stadium and facilities, which were disorderly and drab, were immediately cleaned up and coated in Hawkeye black and gold. The Tigerhawk logo and Hawkeye Marketing Company were introduced, and black-and-gold apparel and novelties were soon being sold in stores across the state.

That same year, the Pittsburgh Steelers won their third Super Bowl in five seasons. They were winners, and Hayden wanted to capitalize on the fact that Iowa shared their colors of black and gold. With a phone call, the Hawkeyes were given permission to copy the Steelers uniforms, and they thrilled fans by starting the 1979 season with a new image. Hayden knew how important appearance was in developing a winning attitude. "At least when we ran out on the field," he remarked, "we would look like winners."

I'd like to say that all of this translated into an immediate winning record. It didn't. But Iowa—not just the university, but the entire state—knew something was different; there was a new energy in the Kinnick parking lot. In 1981, the winning attitudes finally translated into a winning season. Hayden's Hawkeyes were off and running to the Big Ten title and the first of many Rose Bowl bids. The rest, as they say, is history.

Experiencing the Hawkeyes' climb to success was a thrilling experience. I'll never forget the first time I saw Hayden walk onto the field with those aviator sunglasses and snakeskin cowboy boots on. What a statement. After a few losses at Iowa, fans began mocking him from the stands. "Okay, Bob Commings," they'd shout. "Take off the glasses. We know it's you in there." (Bob Commings coached the Hawkeyes during the five years prior to Hayden's arrival and left with an unpopular record of

18–37.) Hayden never flinched. A couple of losses and a few angry fans were not going to change his commitment to winning or his confidence in his team's ability to do so. He never stopped looking, acting, or talking like a winner.

About the same time that Hayden started coaching at Iowa, I was working through the necessary pains of becoming a successful entrepreneur. Although I didn't have to endure the same public criticism that Hayden did, I still had my critics and still had to overcome unfavorable odds. About 75 percent of new business start-ups make it through the first year, 50 percent are still alive after five years, and only 30 percent of companies are thriving after ten years. So, why did I want to challenge such long odds? Partly for the same reason Hayden enjoyed turning

Photo Credit: UIowa Photo Service

Coach Fry

Tom's father, Jerry Berthel, holding Tom as a baby

losing football programs into winners: to prove it could be done. More personally, though, I was inspired by my parents.

While I was growing up, I saw my father do whatever it took to make his electrical business succeed. He worked long hours and didn't take many vacations. When business was slow he took side jobs, driving a tractor at times to make ends meet. His business never made us rich, but it met the basic needs of thirteen children and a wife . . . somewhat of a miracle. Our family struggled, yet we could be looked at as a success.

When I observed my father, I saw a hard worker who was self-taught. He never threw his hands up in defeat or let us kids see him discouraged. He wasn't a great communicator, but he worked hard to provide for us and never let us wonder if we were going to have enough money for groceries. I admired that like crazy. There were times when I hoped to own part of my dad's company, but I became impatient and opted for college and the investment business instead. Still, my father's example provided me with the inspiration I needed to start and grow my

Berthel family

own company. Dad enjoyed the freedom of being his own boss and the unlimited potential of owning his own business. Those are things I wanted, too.

Not long after I graduated from college, my father was diagnosed with lung cancer, which he succumbed to shortly thereafter. This was undoubtedly the result of his tremendous smoking habit. Dad smoked hand-rolled, unfiltered cigarettes right out of the Prince Albert can. I remember him pointing to a particular symbol on the can when I was a young boy and asking me if I knew what it meant. I didn't understand it at the time, but it was a skull and crossbones—the symbol of death.

I had always seen my mother as an amazing woman, but never so much as in the months and years that surrounded Dad's death. Mom was pregnant for thirteen of my first eighteen years, yet kept our home and family running smoothly and constantly modeled the importance of loving and caring for one another. I'll never forget our trips to the grocery store when I was a kid. Mom was either pregnant or toting a new baby and pushing a cart full of food while she made sure the rest of us were minding our manners. She sacrificed for her family and was always a picture of strength, but my dad's illness and death put new and greater demands on her life.

Not only did she have several children still at home to care for, but the family business had always been dependent on Dad for survival, so she had to go to work to make ends meet. In addition to raising children and working, Mom regularly drove from Delmar to Iowa City, ninety minutes each way, to support her husband while he was slowly deteriorating in the hospital. The most amazing part of it all was her quiet determination to do what needed to be done. She never complained of the pain and loneliness she surely felt. She never let the adversity of life beat her. Instead, she displayed a positive attitude in the midst of extraordinary struggle. She never stopped looking, acting, or talking like a winner, and her example has given me the confidence to model a winning attitude for my own family, employees, and customers.

Family can be a strange animal. Family members often disagree on things and sometimes fail to recognize one another's strengths and weaknesses. We spend hours and hours making business and career plans, but often neglect to set goals for our own family. Still, as hard as it may be to stick together at times, family is invaluable. We learn so much from our loved ones, and how we choose to nurture (or ignore) those relationships will shape our

Berthel Fisher sign at Kinnick Stadium

outlook on life, and can impact our community and even our world. Valuing family can lead to a great sense of personal well-being, and carrying the value of family into the business world can lead to a great deal of corporate success as well.

Growing a new company is an uphill battle. In the face of unfavorable odds, I have had to convince those around me that everything is going to be okay—that we are going to win—even when it doesn't feel that way. Just like Hayden's first days at Iowa and my parents' attitude toward the challenges of life, a losing mind-set cannot be tolerated.

Largely due to the influence of the role models in my life, my determination paid off, and within a few years Berthel Fisher & Company was off the ground and experiencing some success. Even so, to capitalize on our initial momentum we needed to expand our customer base by exposing our services to a larger regional area. This would be tricky. We were holding our own, but all of our profit was being used to cover our basic operating costs and modest salaries. Needless to say, advertising dollars could not be wasted.

It was during this phase of our company's growth that I was approached by the University of Iowa's Athletic Department, presenting Berthel Fisher & Company the opportunity to become a corporate sponsor. In exchange for our sponsorship, we would receive prime advertising space in the football and basketball stadiums and on the annual coaches' show, and one

Berthel Fisher sign at Carver Hawkeye Arena

of the Hawkeye coaches would provide a motivational speech at our company's annual convention.

I never doubted the value of the offer; it was just the sort of exposure we were looking for. Not only would the advertisements be seen by folks from our own area, but also by alumni, fans, and opposing fans from across Iowa and throughout the Midwest. Even though it seemed like a no-brainer, as far as advertising was concerned it required us to take a substantial financial risk. It was a risk we decided to take, and I'll never forget the first time I saw our Berthel Fisher sign right next to the Coca-Cola billboard in Kinnick Stadium. I was blown away. It looked amazing. With one decision we were suddenly in the same league as Coca-Cola—at least, it looked that way.

People began confirming this perception immediately. "Wow, you guys have really hit the big time!" "Congratulations—you've obviously arrived!" As they say, perception is everything.

The buzz created by the billboard exceeded my expectations, and soon it was time for the promised coach's speech to be delivered at our annual convention. About forty of our employees and brokers gathered at the Colony Village in the quaint town of Little Amana, Iowa, to hear Coach Fry speak. I had no idea what to expect. I knew he was a football hero, but what would he have to say to a roomful of investment brokers?

As I shook Hayden's hand and welcomed him to the convention, I was a bit intimidated by his John Wayne stature and celebrity status. Even so, his quick wit and Texas charm put me at ease, and he quickly secured his place in the Berthel Fisher family. One thing that was clear from the moment he entered the room: He wasn't there to promote himself. He was there to help us win—period.

Hayden and Tom at Hayden's first BFC Annual Convention

Not only did it prove to be a good marketing decision, but becoming a corporate sponsor of the University of Iowa also turned out to be one of the most defining decisions in the history of the company, as well as for me, personally. It established a winning image for Berthel Fisher and gave birth to one of the most important friendships of my life.

While I didn't realize it at the time, I see now that I was doing the same thing with my company that Hayden had done with his football team. The Hawkeyes were certainly not in the same league as the Pittsburgh Steelers. They were amateurs who hadn't yet won a game, but wearing a winning uniform made the players, coaches, and fans think like winners, and that attitude translated into a winning record. Likewise, when we displayed our first billboard at the university, Berthel Fisher & Company wasn't

Tom golfing with Hayden at the Amana golf course

anywhere close to being in the same league with Coca-Cola, but the winning image it created propelled us to the next level of success in the investments industry.

Human nature is a funny thing when it comes to ego. We are drawn to the "glitz," and we feel a sense of importance when we sit in the front-row seat or rub shoulders with a celebrity. It makes us feel good about ourselves and gets our "ambition juices" flowing. This is why healthy role models are so important. No one is perfect, but those in the spotlight, like Hayden, must always strive to do the right thing. Everyone is influenced by role models (especially children), and great care should be taken by politicians, sports figures, and business leaders to set the right example for future generations.

Hindsight may be twenty-twenty, but the key to inspiring belief is looking forward and keeping your nose clean. Success will come when you look past the obstacles and inspire optimism in others—looking, acting, and talking like a winner before you've ever won a game.

POSTGAME WITH COACH FRY

Looking like a winner

This chapter fires me up. It's so true. Everyone watches the leader, and if the leader isn't offering a clear and confident vision, then they'll never get it done.

I think it's the reason so many Americans are demoralized today. The big guys and gals in Washington are selling the idea that government is the answer to all our problems. Government will make us winners again. As a result, we have a crisis of disbelief. Young people are forgetting that the foundation of our nation's success is made up of the hard work and contributions of individuals. We are a nation of unlimited potential, but that potential is being snuffed out because individual contributions and personal responsibility are swiftly being replaced with government programs and dependency. As a result, too many people aren't taking ownership of their own destiny; too many don't truly believe that they have the personal ability and responsibility to be winners.

That's the reason I went to Iowa City. I saw fans and football players who had forgotten their individual winning potential. They'd become satisfied with close losses. Can you imagine?

Satisfied with losing? It boggled my mind. I saw people hungry for a little sizzle.

As soon as I arrived in Iowa City, I got to work changing the way the Hawkeyes viewed themselves. No more losing. I noticed that fans from all the really outstanding teams in the nation were decked out in their school colors on game day. Nebraska was a sea of crimson, Notre Dame was doused in blue and gold, and it was time for Iowa fans to follow suit—to look like a unified team from the parking lot to the locker room.

Mini Hawkeyes with the Iowa cheerleaders

We started Hawkeye Marketing Company, hiring Jim Quinn to handle sales and Bill Colbert to do design. Everything we made and sold was black and gold and stamped with the new Tigerhawk logo. Before long, our stadium looked like the home of a successful football team.

With the fans outfitted, it was time to equip the team. Joe Greene, a former player from North Texas, played for the Pittsburgh Steelers at the time, so I gave him a call. We were very fortunate to share the Steelers colors, and I asked Joe for permission to copy their uniforms. He got me in touch with their equipment guy who transferred me to one of the team's executives. I explained who I was, that Iowa hadn't had a winning season in nearly two decades, and that I'd like the boys to start seeing themselves as winners again. They were honored to oblige, and three days later I received Terry Bradshaw's uniform in the mail.

We measured every element of the jersey, from the width of the stripes to the spaces in between, to be sure everything was duplicated exactly. It was really exciting for me, and my equipment people at Iowa were just elated.

As cool as the new uniforms looked, there was nothing magical about them. Inside each jersey and under each helmet were the same guys I'd started out with, but they were beginning to believe. I could see it in their eyes. When their hard work and authentic accomplishments on the practice field united with their new "Super Bowl" look, something special happened, and we started to make an entire state believe that the Iowa Hawkeyes could win again.

Photo Credit: UIowa Photo Service

Coach Fry with Tigerhawk logo in background

It's important for me to stop here for just a minute and clarify what I mean by *winning*. As a Big Ten football coach and a highly competitive individual, winning ball games is important to me. It is a great thrill to see a team rewarded with a win after weeks of hard practice, and I'd never pretend not to love it. Still, winning goes far beyond the score of any game. It's about what each player and coach learns along the way, and what mental and physical adjustments are made to increase the team's success. Good leaders always find a little win in every loss.

In fact, some of our best learning experiences came out of games that we lost. Maybe our players gave an outstanding effort against a much more talented football team, and played them close the whole way. Maybe there were great improvements made by a particular player from the week before. My coaches and I looked at film after every loss, specifically identifying sources of positive motivation.

In 1970, when I was coaching at SMU, seventy Marshall University football players, coaches, and fans lost their lives in a plane crash in West Virginia. It was impossible to wrap my mind around the severe loss Marshall had to deal with, and I couldn't help but wonder how the leaders of the university would pick up the pieces and bring healing to the Marshall family. With a grieving town and a hodgepodge team, Jack Lengyel was hired to coach the new Thundering Herd. He coached the four years following the crash and left Marshall in 1974 with a record of 9–33, but he left a winner. Simply because he kept the program alive and kept playing the game, the human spirit was restored and Marshall began to heal. Winning games was not the measure of his success. His success—their success—was found in restoring the belief that life must go on, and that we must keep on living it.

Photo Credit: Ted Roeder

Hawkeye celebration

The simple truth is that nobody wants to lose. Nobody wants to fail. So, when a demoralized young man, or young lady, is down on his or her luck and losing faith, I suggest you start selling a little sizzle. There is a winner in every person; there is always something worth fighting for. I truly believe that, and sometimes a little positive motivation is all that's needed in order for people to believe in themselves again. Not empty praise or shallow victories, but good coaching. I've never seen a coach or player yet who didn't rise to the occasion and take ownership of his own success once he began to hear the sizzle.

3

ONLY HIRE HEAD COACHES

Recruiting the whole person

OBSTACLES ARE INEVITABLE. Wherever you happen to be in your business or personal life, regardless of how wonderful things may look at the moment, challenges remain on the horizon. It's a fact of life. Though we may not be able to control the future as much as we would like, we *can* control the sort of people we have on our team when adversity comes our way.

In 2001, following the attacks on the World Trade Center, the United States and world markets experienced record losses. The New York Stock Exchange, the American Stock Exchange, and the NASDAQ remained closed for a week, resulting in a 1,369.7-point drop in the Dow Jones Industrial Average, and a $1.4 trillion loss in stock values. Many people felt dazed and confused about their financial future. *War* became a buzzword

Tom with Berthel Fisher COO CFO Ron Brendengen

for the first time since the Gulf War; who could have known that this was just a warm-up for what was to come a few years later?

While the financial industry took a hit, our company survived—in part, because of shrewd business decisions and a high degree of diversification. But we also survived the epic economic fallout because we refused to partner with paycheck players.

My chief financial officer Ron and I were in Atlanta for a regional meeting when the attacks occurred. We had flown from Cedar Rapids to Chicago and on to Norfolk, Virginia, the day before, and I was scheduled to fly to Washington, D.C., on the afternoon of September 11th.

As I reached the lobby, preparing to leave for our meetings, I noticed my colleagues glued to news coverage on the television. I heard one say that a plane had crashed into one of the World Trade Center buildings. After a few quiet minutes of watching the smoke rise, Ron said, "I don't think that was an accident. Look how clear it is." As I watched

Brandon, Hayden, and Paige in the early years

in shock, it made me wonder. We went ahead and left for our meetings, completely unaware that a short time later, additional planes would crash and our world would be changed forever.

As things unfolded, I called my wife Deanna. Both of us were sad and amazed, and our thoughts turned to our children, who could have been called to defend our country. Standing in a hotel garden next to a fountain on a beautiful morning, many emotions swept over me. After years of prosperity and peace, America now faced fear and uncertainty.

Not able to fly home, Ron and I kept our rental car and headed out of Atlanta, stocked with food and bottled water since we didn't know how supplies might be affected. It was absolutely surreal listening to radio coverage of the day's events as we made the twelve-hour drive to Iowa. One gas station attendant proclaimed that Armageddon had arrived.

The events of 9/11 are forever locked in my mind. I am so grateful for the men and women who have given their lives to defend our homeland from further attack. Years later, many are still sacrificing their own comfort and security for our protection.

In the days immediately following the attack, I called a meeting with the leaders of every department at Berthel Fisher. The boardroom was silent, and I knew I needed to lead like never before. Not only were the men and women in the room faced with business-related anxiety, but we were all faced with personal fears as well. What happens to my eighteen-year-old son if the draft is reinstated? Is my family safe from additional attacks? In the midst of devastating loss and uncertainty, we all had to be strong. I had to convey a sense of confidence and clear direction.

The coming months and years would require great sacrifice and tough decisions. I knew, without a doubt, that my coworkers were up to the task. They followed my lead and ran with it, creating greatness in the company while fighting a historic three-year financial downturn. These motivated men and women, with their spirits of optimism and commitment to living and working with integrity, contributed profoundly to our stability and growth in the years that followed.

Early in our friendship, Hayden began sharing his hiring philosophy with me. "In thirty-eight years as a head coach," he told me, "I never hired an assistant coach unless I was completely convinced that he was motivated to become a head coach. If you're going to be a winner, you have to surround yourself with winners."

In 1981, when looking for an assistant coach to fill the line position at Iowa, Hayden had many qualified applicants to consider. They included former head coaches from college teams and some who had coached in the NFL. Most human resources managers would have been impressed with such a great field of candidates. Hayden saw it differently. To him, talent and experience were only a piece of the hiring puzzle.

Coach Jimmy Johnson, who played for Arkansas during Hayden's assistant coaching days under Frank Broyles, was coaching at the University of Pittsburgh and learned of Hayden's search for a line coach. He recommended a guy named Kirk Ferentz, who Hayden later brought to Iowa for an interview. Despite Kirk's comparatively inferior résumé, Hayden saw his sincere ambition to become a head coach.

As a result, he hired Kirk on the spot. Hayden knew that Kirk would be dedicated and that he would study every aspect of the game. He would be ethical and recruit within the rules, and he would see that his players graduated.

The gamble paid off. Not only was Kirk Ferentz a successful assistant coach

Hayden and Kirk Ferentz

45

with Hayden for nine seasons, but he also went on to become Iowa's head coach after Hayden's retirement in 1998, leading the Hawkeyes to appearances in six consecutive bowl games.

This is just one of many success stories. In his years of coaching, Hayden had many assistant coaches go on to become head coaches for high school programs and over twenty assistants become head coaches of college or professional teams: Oklahoma's Bob Stoops, Iowa State's Dan McCarney, Kansas State's Bill Snyder, Chuck Long at San Diego State, Barry Alvarez at Wisconsin, Nebraska's Bo Pelini, Don Paterson at Western Illinois, Wisconsin's Brett Bielema, Jerry Moore at Appalachian State, Dave Smith at SMU, and Arizona's Mike Stoops . . . to name a few.

Following Hayden's lead, I surround myself with head-coach types at Berthel Fisher. Whether choosing friends, business partners, or employees, I have learned to look past people's accomplishments—past their résumés—to the bigger picture of how they conduct their lives. What sort of character does the person have? What are his/her personal and professional ambitions? Does his/her attitude fit with my philosophy and mission? Do I enjoy spending time with the person?

Hayden consistently affirms that talent is secondary to the overall characteristics of a person, and I am convinced that our company avoids many problems and deficiencies by evaluating every potential team member as a whole person rather than basing hiring decisions on isolated skills and talents.

We want people who are talented, of course, but we also want men and women of integrity. We want "room-brighteners." Hayden often recalls the charisma of Pro Football Hall of

Famer Doak Walker, and the effect he had on those around him. "When Doak entered the locker room," Hayden says, "it became brighter. He didn't have to have his football uniform on. He wasn't running for a touchdown. He was the most humble, quiet person in the world, but there was something about him that just turned the lights on when he entered a room."

As a president and CEO, this personality trait is incredibly important to me. It's impossible to quantify the value of assembling a team of pleasant and positive people, but one thing is certain: A team of room-brighteners creates an authentic winning culture that promotes optimism, regardless of the day's stock market reports. Let me be clear: I am not interested in hiring folks to stand around and tell me how wonderful I am, or to congratulate each other for showing up. What I do look for are team members who have a spirit of hope and a genuine appreciation for the talents and diversity of others. Our bottom line consistently increases as we surround ourselves with team members who see money as a by-product of honesty and hard work, not as a primary focus.

Each time we interview a broker or prospective employee who is interested in joining our company, I make it clear that our first priority is to care for the best interests of our team members and clients. The cutthroat, win-at-any-cost mentality of Wall Street has no place in our company's mission. Even though there are many success stories on Wall Street, making money at any cost is not one of them. There is more to our team members and clients than their bank accounts.

As a result, our profits increase year after year because we have a team of like-minded people who genuinely enjoy one another's

BFC President Emeritus Dwight Wheelan and BFC COO CFO Ron Brendengen

company and are deeply committed to winning. If that is the sort of opportunity the registered representative is looking for, then we welcome him/her with open arms and do everything possible to support his/her success. Otherwise, I wish the individual the best in the future and we go our separate ways. When we believe we have found a good team member, we know they will be there when we need them the most.

One of our Texas representatives recently talked with me about his early work experience with a financial "big house," as he called it. "It was high pressure from the start," he told me, "and all about the money." He went on to explain an aggressive interview process and a work environment that was much more focused on ensuring the firm's success than growing a team of successful individuals. The fundamental reason for his displeasure with his previous employer, in my interpretation, is that he felt no ownership in what he was doing, and didn't feel valued as a whole, dynamic person.

Perhaps the biggest hindrance to building a team of talented, respectable, room-brighteners is that the leader is likely to lose his/her position as the smartest, most likable person in the room. That is the very reason so many leaders shy away from hiring head-coach types. They become threatened by the abilities and successes of others instead of embracing them.

Hayden's hiring philosophy for his football programs had everything to do with celebrating the strengths of others. He recognized that the most important step in creating winning teams was to select exceptional individuals and then empower them to grow and succeed. Hayden masterfully maintained an "If you're successful, I'm successful" attitude, and continues to believe that too many teams, in football and business, fail because leaders are unwilling to embrace the talents and gifts of team members as a great asset instead of a great threat.

When discussing the issue of assembling a team of exceptional leaders, Hayden tells a story of doing chores on his family's farm as a young boy. One morning, his father instructed him to take their pickup truck, fill it with hay, and deliver the hay to the cows in the field. Now, the farm consisted of nearly 800 acres of hills, trees, and streams, and the cows were allowed to freely graze the property. "Daddy," Hayden protested, "I'll never be able to find all those cows. They could be anywhere out there." His father reassured him that the task was much simpler than he was making it out to be. All he had to do was drive the truck out in the field, stop, get out, and listen for the sound of a bell.

Before letting the cattle roam free, Hayden's father observed them carefully to determine which cow emerged as the leader,

"Ringing the cowbell" at Soldier Field, Chicago

and then he hung a cowbell around the leader's neck. "When you find the bell cow," he told Hayden, "you'll find the whole herd." It didn't take long for Hayden to hear the clanging of the bell as he drove through the field. Sure enough, he easily located the bell cow, which was surrounded by the entire herd—just as his dad had predicted.

The bell-cow concept stuck with Hayden and became an integral part of his coaching routine. Though it manifested itself most directly in the way he engaged his players, it was also reflected in his hiring philosophy. He looked for natural leaders, head-coach types, who were successful individuals with the ability to motivate others. Once on the team, these individuals were provided with clear expectations of what was required of them in order to win. They were given a theoretical cowbell, empowering them

Speaking at BFC Annual Convention

with a great deal of freedom to exercise authority and creativity within their area of responsibility.

Sitting at a cloth-draped table at the Marriott in Coralville, Iowa, surrounded by hundreds of Berthel Fisher employees and representatives, I couldn't help but think of how Hayden's bell-cow initiative has influenced my own hiring and management practices. It was the week of our annual convention, and I felt privileged to be listening to four of our registered representatives as they shared their personal game plans for success: how they recruit new clients, care for existing ones, and manage their business in the midst of a fragile economy.

About the only thing these representatives from Kansas, Texas, New York, and Missouri have in common is a huge sense of motivation and a great deal of integrity. Each one has a completely different approach to growing and maintaining a successful investment business, and each enjoys a great deal of ownership and success.

Rich, from Kansas, focuses on assisting a primarily blue-collar clientele as they navigate the investment and tax worlds, while John uses his background as a CPA to help small and midsize businesses manage their employee investment programs in Missouri. In Texas, Michael works to accommodate the individual needs of his clients, while Dan, from New York, prefers a more uniform money-management approach. Even though their specific business practices vary, their messages are consistent: "Be the sort of person that people trust with their money."

In today's world, transparency is more important than ever. People want to know where their money is and who has control of it. The Madoff scandal has shocked the investment world and raised a lot of questions. Who could do such a thing, and why? Unfortunately, Madoff's tactics will have lasting implications for the entire industry, including those who do things with integrity.

As I listened, I realized that the panelists represented the effectiveness of growing our team based on whole-person characteristics rather than isolated skills. Because I am confident in the integrity and ability of our representatives, I am also confident in hanging a theoretical cowbell around their necks and sending them out with the freedom to exercise independent thinking and creativity.

We are not cattle farmers or football players, but we have assembled a team of bell cows at Berthel Fisher nonetheless. They are successful, and that makes our company successful. Our team is composed of men and women of integrity who, at the very core of their beings, are committed to success. As a result, our representatives and support staff display great internal consistency when faced with external turmoil, and our executive team truly respects their authority. Our continuing challenge, as with all companies, is to grow and maintain a healthy culture, maintain and monitor that integrity, and find appropriate bell cows to help lead.

So many problems are prevented when hiring decisions are based on the characteristics of the whole person. When adversity does come, head-coach types and room-brighteners are not easily discouraged. Instead, they face problems with determination and optimism, and as a result, the entire team is more successful. The head coach is able to concentrate on the big-picture strategy rather than expending energy putting out trivial fires that can lead to disaster. Words cannot adequately describe the freedom I feel as a leader, knowing that our company is in the hands of men and women of integrity who take ownership in their individual success, and, therefore, the overall success of the company. They are also charged with maintaining that integrity for the good of the company.

Beyond Xs and Os

Tom Berthel with Ron Brendengen and Fred Fisher

54

POSTGAME WITH COACH FRY

Only hire head coaches

I trusted my assistant coaches and greatly respected each of them. We were (and still are) like a family. Even though I tried to hire people that were better than me, I never felt threatened by their talents or successes. The only thing I felt for them was a great sense of happiness when things went right for them. So many of those guys have gone on to become head coaches and managers, and I am just so proud of every one of them.

In order to inspire effective leadership among the coaching staff, I needed to communicate a clear game plan. As the head coach, it was my responsibility to make decisions about what was required to win—on and off the field—and to define the sort of character that was expected. Each season, I presented these things very clearly to the coaching staff at each position. They heard what we were going to do and how we were going to do it. Clear direction was given on defense and offense, training rules, and even what to wear. Once they understood precisely what I expected and we had established mutual trust, then I listened to their suggestions. When one of them came to me with an idea, I'd simply say, "Coach, this is your baby." Once they knew I trusted them, they began to use their experience and ideas to make the team better. This is what made the winning difference.

When you hire head-coach types, independent thinkers who are well prepared to do the job, it's an insult to get in their way. When a coach came up with an idea to improve our operation, we'd try it. If it worked, wonderful; if not, I'd explain why it wasn't working (so that everyone completely understood what was behind my decision), and then we'd eliminate it.

Giving my coaches a great deal of ownership never led to power struggles, and I never felt threatened by their abilities, because no one ever questioned who the boss was. There is great security and freedom in knowing who's in charge. It's not an ego trip. It's simply necessary in creating a focused team.

The U.S. Marine Corps deserves much of the credit for my leadership philosophy. Being a marine taught me the significance of structure and discipline, the lifesaving power of solid trust in the ranks, and the importance of having a game plan for everything. I was able to take what I learned in the Corps and use it in my career as a head football coach. What a rewarding experience

2nd Lieutenant John Hayden Fry, USMC, 1953

it was. We worked hard, we trusted one another, and we experienced so many victories together. My assistant coaches are like part of my family, wonderful guys who worked so hard to improve our players far beyond the Xs and Os of football.

I hired Kirk Ferentz ahead of other outstanding, skilled applicants because of his ability to organize and communicate. During the interview process, Kirk explained things to me in such a clear way, and I really appreciated his high ethical standards on and off the football field. He's gone on to do so much for Iowa as head coach.

So many others became head coaches and managers. Ted Thompson became the general manager of the Green Bay Packers. Harold Richardson became the general manager of the Atlanta Falcons. The Stoops brothers are head coaches, with Mike at Arizona and Bobby setting all sorts of records at Oklahoma. The only thing I don't like about mentioning any of my coaches is the certainty of leaving others out. They are all just like my sons, regardless of where they've landed.

Here's the bottom line: The head-coach types that I hired, who employed their creativity and contributed to the program, were recognized and rewarded verbally and monetarily (when possible). A leadership team who capitalizes on a diverse collection of experiences, talents, and ideas—and respects the authority of the head coach—is virtually unstoppable. Regardless of how strong I may be as head coach, my own experiences, talents, and ideas are never enough without the contributions of others.

Photo Credit: Ted Roeder

Iowa Coach Kirk Ferentz

There are so many variables in coaching, as in any leadership situation, and some of the biggest critics are folks who have never played the game. When my leadership, or that of my coaches, was called into question, I always remembered the words of wisdom I heard from my good friend John Wayne, who said, "Don't ever judge another person until you have stood in his moccasins."

Looking back, one of my greatest accomplishments was my ability to recruit staff and players based on the whole person—not just their talent on the field, but the emphasis they placed on playing the game with integrity, helping others to become successful, conducting themselves as men of character, and striving for a quality education.

Hiring head-coach types is a vital part of anticipating adversity. Not only did it establish a productive culture, but it also made my job a lot more fun. We worked hard together, played hard together, and we never, ever doubted our ability to win together.

4

KNOWING "SPOT"

Building intentional relationships

WHEN A COLLEGE football player pulls on a pair of gym shorts and a T-shirt, preparing for his first day of fall practice, he's probably thinking about speed and agility drills, and anticipating the intense plyometrics, strength training, and conditioning that await him. Coach Fry (or "Coach Freud," as he is often called) had different plans for his players' first day of practice.

Hayden started every football season with psychology, not sweat. The first days of fall practice were spent defining what it takes to win, on and off the field, and creating a team committed to helping one another succeed. According to Hayden, it wasn't rocket science. "We simply listed the things that were required to win and the things that would cause us to lose. Then, each player had a choice to make."

Players participated in mental drills rather than physical ones. They were asked to stand and share something about themselves with their teammates. What is something you value in your life? What positive personal experience has made you a winner? Some players shared stories about school; some spoke about football or situations with family members or friends, and some shared stories of faith. The exact substance of the stories wasn't really the important thing; the objective was to establish transparency among members and, with three consecutive nights of sharing, to achieve authentic and essential camaraderie.

Sharing pieces of ourselves with others creates an immediate personal investment. It gives us a reason to help each other become successful. Our relationships develop substance beyond simply being members of the same team. As a result, our individual talents and abilities multiply and put us in a position where we are more likely to succeed.

Early in my career, there were two men who really helped me to understand the value of Coach Fry's relationship-building strategy. Because I was just starting out in the insurance and investment business, my only real teammates were my customers. For me to be successful, they had to be successful.

Every time I called on Arnold, a longtime farmer and one of my first customers, his wife would bring out a pitcher of lemonade and the three of us would sit on their front porch, visiting and enjoying the views on their beautiful Iowa farm. I learned about their kids and their farming business. I learned how deeply they both valued owning and working their land. We laughed and talked, and our conversation was never rushed. These were my teammates, and I was there to invest in them and to ask them to invest in me.

At some point in the conversation, I would ask Arnold about the status of his estate planning, and we would talk about his priorities and how he wanted his assets to be transferred to his children in an orderly, uncomplicated manner. I learned long ago that financial products are only a means to satisfy a need or want. Arnold knew his children and grandchildren would be well taken care of financially, but he wanted to protect them as best he could, and to preserve family relationships without allowing money to get in the way. He trusted me to assist him in that effort.

Some folks, especially those in the business of personal finance, may view these long talks on the front porch as a waste of time. But to me, they provide an avenue toward establishing the same authentic and essential camaraderie with my customers that Hayden worked so hard to develop among his players. Arnold knew I liked him. I enjoyed our visits and genuinely cared about his family. And, because he trusted me, he began to do more and more to help me grow my business.

Every time we bumped into one another in town or at the country club, Arnold asked what more I could do for him. He was always looking to buy something, sincerely wanting to help the young, twenty-something salesman who took the time to stop by for a front-porch visit and a glass of lemonade. In a world of cell phones and e-mail, the power of a heartfelt, face-to-face conversation should never be underestimated.

Another customer who significantly impacted my early career was a wealthy businessman who I became acquainted with through a building project. Everyone in our community was aware that Ed had a lot of money, so he was no stranger to salesmen or requests for charity. In fact, I'm quite sure he had plenty of opportunities to buy insurance and investments from more experienced representatives. Even so, he and I had worked side by side on several projects, and he seemed to admire my willingness to roll up my sleeves and get involved. We spent time getting to know one another, and I came to truly admire all he had accomplished.

I never really gave Ed a sales pitch. We developed a friendship and he trusted me, so he began coming to me for investment advice. "What do you think I should do for my grandchildren?" he'd ask. "Can you help me figure out what to do with a particular account?" Before I knew it, and much to my amazement, Ed became one of my biggest customers, and we began trading business ideas on a regular basis.

One afternoon, he stopped by my office unexpectedly and was clearly upset. He had just come from a bank board meeting, of which he was a member, and had learned that I was attempting to get a loan in order to purchase a new building for our company. Ed shared his disappointment that I had not been comfortable enough to request the loan from him directly. Not only could he give me a better interest rate, but he was also authentically interested in helping me to achieve my goals. He knew how difficult it was to get a new business off the ground. Long story short, I worked with my attorney, accepted Ed's loan, and worked hard to repay it promptly. Wow. If I had treated Ed as "just another customer," I never would have enjoyed the blessing of his friendship or the many ways he assisted me in business over the years. Darell Rettig, Tom Ray, and many others in the community of Maquoketa also helped me forward my career in those days.

Berthel Fisher's first building—Downtown, Cedar Rapids

Building intentional relationships with customers, business partners, and employees assists me in managing the psychology of my company's proverbial locker room. It helps me to identify and train leaders according to individual strengths, and creates an atmosphere of trust and teamwork. Most important, knowing our team members on a personal level gives me the confidence and information I need to delegate effectively. I know who is best suited to handle particular projects and who needs additional training. I know when to be a bit more patient due to an individual's health or family struggle. In turn, team members are loyal and hardworking, and they view success as a collective venture. You win; I win.

When Hayden first arrived in Iowa, he had to change the Hawkeyes' long-held losing mentality. He had to change the total environment, from the players' conduct on down to their attitude in the classroom and their way of relating to one another. He was committed to rebuilding the total athlete and reconstructing a winning value system.

Some coaches know the game, but they don't know people. Hayden knows people. Any coach can create good plays and techniques, but if he isn't able to teach, communicate, and help players execute them, it's not going to work. Hayden once told me, "If one of my players had a dog named 'Spot,' then I knew all about Spot. I knew his family, I knew about his girlfriend, I knew about his personal struggles, and I knew where he was on Friday night." This open-door policy cultivated an atmosphere of trust with his players and assistant coaches. They knew he was honest and sincere, so they received his instruction wholeheartedly and were less likely to break his rules. As a result, Hayden was able to maximize the team's success on the field by celebrating strengths and confronting weaknesses. "Because I knew my kids," Hayden says, "I could throw out what a kid couldn't do, instead of throwing out the whole kid."

This philosophy can be very useful for companies as they examine their operations. What is each employee's strength? Where do they shine? What are their weaknesses? How can they be redirected to be the most effective? Oftentimes, when a coach changes a player's position or role on the team, the decision is

Iowa versus Michigan, 1985

second-guessed. Fans question why a coach would make such a change when the player has had success in the previous position or role. Later, when the player becomes an All-American and goes on to the NFL, it all makes sense. Knowing the strengths and weaknesses of our players allows us to make those moves.

Thinking outside the box and finding hidden strengths in team members creates excitement in an organization, and it is so much fun when it works. Instead of letting someone struggle in the same role year after year, or simply getting rid of them, a good leader searches for a way to help them blossom in a new role. First and foremost, the team has to trust the coach. Through a relationship of trust, new and exciting worlds open up.

Knowing his players on a deeper level also helped Hayden understand the mental and emotional climate in the locker room. It allowed him to recognize unhealthy tension and determine the best way to minimize it. One of Hayden's most memorable, tension-relieving moments occurred during pregame warm-ups at the 1985 Iowa-Michigan game.

Iowa was ranked number one in the nation and Michigan was ranked number two. Coach Bo Schembechler's Michigan team opened the season with five straight wins, including a 31–0 victory over Michigan State and convincing wins over Notre Dame, South Carolina, Maryland, and Wisconsin. Considering how they finished the previous season with a disappointing 6–6 record, Michigan was fired up to beat the Hawkeyes and reclaim a position of dominance in the Big Ten Conference.

Hayden realized that his players and coaches were under a great deal of pressure to defend their number-one spot, and rumor had it that attendance at Kinnick Stadium would be record-breaking. By Friday afternoon, as Hayden put it, all the hay was in the barn. There would be no more practices before Saturday's game, and he needed to do something to get the team to relax.

Game day arrived. Traditional pregame warm-ups were under way, and Hayden decided to mix things up a bit. He had the guards and centers change places during the punting drills, which meant the guards were snapping balls to the punter for the first time ever. It was a mess. Every time a ball was snapped it flew over the punter's head or bounced on the ground. It wasn't the sort of drill—or performance—anyone expected prior to any game, especially one of such significance.

Well, Coach Schembechler saw the commotion from across the field, shook his head in disbelief, and headed toward the Iowa bench. Seeing him coming, Hayden stood a little taller, folded his arms a little tighter, and never took his eye off the

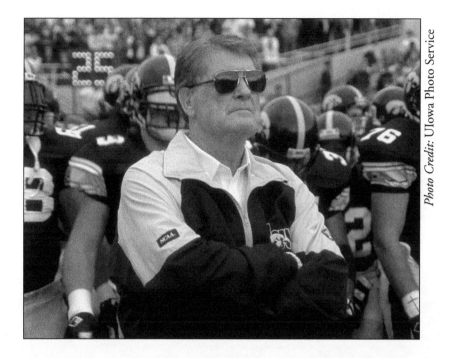

line. "Fry," Schembechler hollered, "you're not gonna let that guy snap during the game, are ya?"

At this, Hayden choked back a smile, turned his head, glanced over the top of his legendary aviator sunglasses, and said, in his most easygoing Texas drawl, "Coach Schembechler, we don't plan on puntin' tonight." And he walked away to another pregame drill.

This sort of amusement was exactly what the Hawkeyes needed to get their minds prepared for the game. They had to stop flirting with the pressure and be reminded of what needed to be done right now. Because Hayden was intentional about getting to know each coach and player personally, from the first day of practice, he knew how to help them get past harmful pressure and prepare them to win psychologically as well as physically.

Incidentally, Iowa beat Michigan 12–10 that day, with a field goal in the final seconds of the game, and went on to become the 1985 Big Ten Conference champs.

When my high school basketball team made it to the 1969 state tournament, it was a "Hoosiers" experience for us. Here we were, a little school with limited funds and talent compared to the schools we would face, and we were definitely feeling the pressure.

At the time, dunking the basketball during a game was against the rules, especially during warm-ups, and it wasn't something we had done before. Our coach realized we needed a little levity

Tom as starting forward for the Delwood Vikings, 34

Delwood Vikings center John Laing

if we were going to perform at our best, and he instructed our center to dunk the ball, knowing it would likely draw a technical foul. Approaching the basket for what we thought would be an uneventful layup, John Laing picked up speed, jumped high, and slammed the ball through the hoop with both hands, swinging his six-foot-eleven frame away from the rim before landing with flare in the middle of the free-throw lane. We all just stood there, stunned. Then, one by one, we let out a battle cry and followed his lead.

Before I knew it, our entire team was in a fired-up frenzy, paying absolutely no attention to the screaming fans or the opposing team. We were in the zone. Turns out, it was exactly what we needed to refocus and prepare ourselves mentally to win. John single-handedly outscored the opposing team, breaking Iowa high school scoring records that night with 68 points.

Whether it's a football coach using personal knowledge about his players to ease pregame tension, a salesperson getting to know the passions and concerns of his customers, or a CEO cultivating honesty and transparency among his team members, the goal is the same. Winning. American author, salesperson, and motivational icon, Zig Ziglar, puts it this way: "You can have everything in life you want if you will just help other people get what they want."

When we take a sincere interest in helping those around us to become winners, the payoff is greater than the profits. In addition to achieving personal success, we experience the joy of friendship, the satisfaction of helping others achieve their dreams, and the multiplying power of teamwork.

POSTGAME WITH COACH FRY

Knowing "Spot"

Bo Schembechler is one of the finest gentlemen I've ever met, and on game day, one of the greatest competitors I've ever coached against. He was a great friend.

Reading Tom's account of the 1985 Iowa-Michigan game brings back so many great memories. Before that game, Schembechler offered me a piece of his trademark sugarless chewing gum. What an opportunity. Instead of simply taking a piece, or politely saying, "No thank you," I snatched the whole pack out of his hand and took off running to our sideline.

I kept that package of chewing gum on my desk for years. Every spring, I went through the upcoming schedule to pick our top three opponents, and then we dedicated a big spring and fall scrimmage to each one in order to keep the players' minds on those teams. Of course, Michigan always made the list, and I always brought out Bo's package of chewing gum when talking to the boys about preparing for the Michigan scrimmage. It took the edge off a bit by humanizing their opponent.

Photo Credit: UIowa Photo Service

Coach Fry with Michigan Coach Bo Schembechler

Building relationships and learning what it takes to motivate people really is the key to living a winning life and leaving a legacy that makes a difference. The reward for taking the time to really know people, without hidden agendas, is a life-time of true friendships and realized dreams.

The greatest joy of my coaching career was getting to know people: talented young athletes, enthusiastic fans, fellow head coaches, an incredible team of assistant coaches, and even entertainers like my good friend Bob Hope, who did several shows for me and was such a wonderful person.

Willie Nelson is another person I really enjoyed meeting. He's just the nicest guy. Back in my North Texas days, Willie did a benefit show for us and then joined us for a down-home Texas barbecue at a friend's ranch following the concert. At the ranch, Willie walked up to me and asked, "Coach Fry, who has my check for the performance?" Well, I had his money in my coat pocket, so I reached in, pulled out a $40,000 check, and handed it to him.

What happened next still amazes me: Willie unfolded the check, asked for a pen, and endorsed it right back to the North Texas Athletic Department. With a wink, he handed it back to me and was on his way. He ended up playing the concert for free.

You know what? The more I associate with successful people, the more I realize that most of them are just the greatest, most down-to-earth folks . . . much more enjoyable than the ones who force themselves on you in order to get ahead. You have to be "real" with people and invest in their lives.

I think one of the reasons my football programs were successful is that we did our homework when recruiting players. We learned about their pets, their hobbies, their friends, what their folks did for a living, about their religion, and what their hopes and dreams were for the future. It made a profound difference. Knowing the "whats" and "whys" of each player's past, present, and future prepared my coaching staff to anticipate his needs and to provide effective leadership on and off the field.

As Tom points out so well, not only do you have to know your own team in order to be successful, but you also have to know your opponents as well. I won three big ball games, against three heavily favored teams, by using their success against them. I studied the teams and knew that they were so confident in their ability to beat us that it would be very difficult for them, mentally, to make adjustments mid-game.

We won all three of those games by taking one of our linemen from the left side and moving him to the right, to outnumber the opponent. In football, this is called an "unbalanced line." Two of the three teams never did make an adjustment. The third team adjusted, but by that point it was too late in the game. Just as I had anticipated, their pride beat them.

The whole point is that you have to do your research in order to win. You have to know your team, your opponent's team, your customers, coworkers, and anyone else that plays a part in your life's game plan.

No amount of money could ever replace the satisfaction I gained from knowing and helping my players. We had kids come in not really knowing right from wrong. To watch them grow and mature—to see them get degrees and go on to be successful in football and in life—was the greatest compensation for all the hours we invested in them.

This is a concept I tried to pass on to our players. I was always looking for leaders. Who was the guy at each position that the other players listened to? Who showed natural leadership tendencies? Those were the guys that became our bell cows. They weren't always the most talented or experienced players, but they were the ones the guys would follow, and they became a great part of our success.

Just like my daddy taught me on the farm: If you want to rally the herd, designate a leader and hang a bell around his neck. Of course, we didn't use cowbells, but I spent a great deal of time with our team leaders, discussing matters of concern and desired direction on and off the field. I found the team listened to the bell cows a whole lot better than the advice of their old coach.

When you take the time to build relationships with people, it is a win-win for everyone. There are so many great people out there, and I've been lucky enough to meet a lot of them. Who is in your life that can help you become successful? Who needs your help in pursuing success? Invest in them. Spend time with them. Take a minute or two to listen to someone else's story, and I guarantee you'll find a great deal of personal fulfillment and satisfaction along the way.

5

MODELING THE WAY

Leading by example

ENTERING THE RECEPTION room on the forty-sixth floor of one of the biggest buildings in downtown Dallas, Hayden was just in time for his noon appointment with H. L. Hunt and still in a state of awe. At that time, in the early 1960s, Hunt had an oil empire worth nearly a billion dollars, making him one of the wealthiest men in the world. Hayden was a young, thirty-something football coach at Southern Methodist University, earning an annual salary of $13,000. What a pair they made.

Upon entering Mr. Hunt's office, Hayden's awe shifted from that of a starry-eyed football coach to that of an interested student. There, behind the desk, was an older gentleman, wearing a wrinkled suit and in obvious need of a haircut. The desk was stacked with books and papers, many of which were spilling over onto the floor. "You're Coach Fry," Hunt said abruptly.

"Yes, sir," Hayden replied, still trying to absorb where he was standing and whose hand he was shaking. Mr. Hunt offered Hayden a chair and then said, "I'm on a pretty tight schedule, son, but would you like to have lunch with me?" Without hesitation, Hayden accepted the invitation, anticipating lunch in the executive boardroom with a maître d' serving the meal. Instead, with no pomp or fanfare, Mr. Hunt reached under his desk to retrieve a brown paper sack. "I hope you like peanut-butter-and-jelly sandwiches," he said. "I was in a big rush to get down here this morning." Still talking, he grabbed a letter opener from his desk that was lying on a stack of papers, cut the sandwich in half, and handed one of the pieces to Hayden.

As you can imagine, the whole thing had Hayden even more amazed and speechless. After a few minutes of eating the sandwich in silence, Mr. Hunt inquired about Hayden's interest in meeting him. In Hayden's usual, candid way, he took a hard swallow and said, "Mr. Hunt, I'm real interested in knowing how you became the richest man in the world."

"Well, son," Hunt replied, "I don't know if that's the fairest statement or not, but I can tell you how I got where I am today." Hayden listened with great expectation. "Number one, you've got to make up your mind what you want to achieve. Number two, you've got to figure out a way to do it. And number three, do it."

Here was a guy who owned more than forty companies and earned nearly a million dollars a week, and yet he was willing to share his sandwich with a stranger and convey his formula for success using no more than a few words. Amazing.

There were two memorable lessons Hayden learned from Mr. Hunt that day. The first was never to forget where you came from. H. L. Hunt had had a modest upbringing and was expected to work hard to contribute to his family's household income. He went on to be a farmhand, lumberjack, and mule skinner before experiencing unprecedented success and wealth in his adult years. Even so, his success didn't appear to change who he was. He lived in a modest home, worked in a modest office, mowed his own lawn, and routinely ate peanut-butter sandwiches from a brown paper bag.

The second lesson Hayden learned is that successful leadership doesn't have to be complicated. Simplicity is powerful. Mr. Hunt's philosophy for success had a significant impact on Hayden's coaching career, causing him to adopt the K-I-S-S (Keep It Simple, Stupid) method when preparing for upcoming games, assimilating wins, and overcoming losses.

Hayden began following Mr. Hunt's advice immediately, determining what his team needed to accomplish, constructing a plan to get it done, and then following the plan. It provided clarity for himself, his assistant coaches, and his players. It set his football teams in a confident and winning direction, helping to minimize unnecessary and counterproductive "clutter."

Still, the best plan in the world is only as successful as the buy-in. Team members must be absolutely convinced that the plan can work before they will give their best effort to the cause. They have to believe, without a doubt, that their leader cares about individual successes as much as the success of the team. They need to see their leader modeling humility, communicating honestly, and accepting personal responsibility when things go wrong.

I don't believe these are new or profound ideas, but they encapsulate the responsibility of leadership and the formula for creating collective buy-in. Effective leaders care more about creating authentic success than obtaining a particular job title or salary.

Early in 2001, there was a lot of discussion about whether or not the U.S. economy was in a recession, and being in the investment business kept it on my mind as well. Hundreds of thousands of jobs were cut in January, putting a strain on family income and hindering economic growth. By June of 2001, with stock prices and consumer confidence falling, the Federal Reserve cut interest rates for the sixth time in six months, hoping to boost consumer spending.

Just prior to the September 11th terrorist attacks, the economy appeared to be stabilizing, and many economists were beginning to express cautious optimism. In fact, in the September 1st issue of *Modern Materials Handling*, Daryl Delano reported, "Although the . . . U.S. economy expanded by an anemic 0.7% during the second quarter of 2001 . . . the fact is that it did grow." He went on to write, "Has the economy hit bottom? We believe so. However, there are still plenty of risks remaining that could undermine what, even under the best of circumstances, is likely to be a fragile recovery. . . ."[1]

Little did Mr. Delano—or any of us, for that matter—know that just ten days after his article was published, our country would sustain a tragic and historic attack. Fear and shock had an immediate impact on consumer spending and the stock market. The "experts" made predictions, and the feds continued to cut interest rates, but the fact of the matter was that nobody knew exactly where it would all end up.

With many businesses floundering and many workers fearing unemployment, it wasn't a time for panic. It was a time for leadership. I knew our employees and business partners shared the shock and fear of their fellow Americans, and, even though it was a promise I couldn't make, I wanted desperately to tell them that everything was going to be all right.

The hard reality was that our company wasn't exempt from the floundering economy of 2001. We experienced the cyclical downturns and the economic impact of 9/11 along with the rest of the world, and I experienced my share of anxiety as the chairman and CEO. While Wall Street began laying people off, I grew more and more determined to sustain our current employee roster. If we were going to survive, we would have to cut spending, and I decided to lead the charge by cutting my own salary by 20 percent. After all, how could I ask my team members to do something that I was unwilling to do myself?

Calling our executive team together, I explained how we could honor our employees and clients by reducing our own salaries to accommodate necessary spending cuts, instead of contributing to a growing unemployment rate. I explained my plan to reduce my salary by 20 percent and asked each of them to join me by doing half as much—reducing their pay by 10 percent.

Upon hearing this proposal, my chief financial officer jumped up immediately and said, "No way. If you're giving up twenty, so am I." I was overwhelmed. One by one, every person in the room joined the effort by cutting their salaries, and we were able to ride out the tough economic times without cutting a single job. After the economy stabilized, we restored their salaries and instituted a bonus plan to pay them back for taking the initiative.

It is my responsibility, as our company's leader, to honor the men and women who work hard to make us successful. It is their dedication that makes us great, not my upbringing or education.

Because they know, without a doubt, that each team member is important to me and that I am willing to authentically shoulder the burdens and responsibilities that come our way, they have been willing to make some remarkable sacrifices themselves.

Several years later, we purchased a company in Ohio that would give us nearly 200 additional offices throughout the U.S. The closing date was set and everything was in order . . . or so I thought. When the date arrived to close the deal, the sellers confessed that they were $500,000 short on the commissions owed to their brokers.

Wanting to salvage the deal, I contacted a couple of friends and was able to borrow $250,000, which amounted to half of the commissions. I went to the top ten producers and said, "Here's the deal. You don't even know me, but I am asking you to trust me. Over the next twelve months, I will be committed to paying you everything you are owed by your old firm. You'll get every nickel you have coming to you, but I'm asking you to stay with me."

Every one of them agreed to stay. They took a risk on me because I took a risk on them. Sometimes you just have to hang in there and ask people to help you shoulder the load. When they see a willingness to sacrifice personal comfort for the sake of the team, they rise to the occasion every time. It's called collective buy-in.

Success is wonderful and winning is fun, but mistakes are inevitable. As CEO of the company, I'll be the first to admit we have made our share of mistakes. We are not perfect with our investment choices and recommendations. Regardless of the talent and dedication of the team, sometimes things go wrong. Hayden experienced amazing success as a football coach. Over the course

of his career, his teams won 232 football games and he collected many entertaining and inspirational stories about winning. Nevertheless, I propose that it is the way Hayden handled losing, not winning, that landed him in the College Football Hall of Fame. In 2003, Deanna and I joined Shirley and others to witness the Hall of Fame ceremony, with Hayden and Jerry LeVias at the Waldorf Astoria in New York City—another unbelievable experience.

It's no secret that Hayden hates to lose. What kind of football coach doesn't? He hates to lose, and he spent every waking moment preparing himself, his assistant coaches, and his players to win. Hayden came to Iowa in 1979 intent on turning a losing football program into a winning one, and he did just that. However, the first couple of seasons were a bit rocky. The worst of his losses came early in the 1980 season, when Nebraska beat the Hawkeyes, 57–0. When Hayden was interviewed after the game, he summed up the loss Texas-style, saying, "We just got blown out of the tub. We played extremely poor football. We coached poorly, and it was obvious that we prepared poorly."

His response provides great insight into his leadership style. Hayden took full responsibility for losses, dealt with mistakes and shortcomings honestly, and then moved on. He had no time for excuses and no time for finger-pointing. After suffering Iowa's worst loss in decades, it must have been tempting to hide behind the mistakes of others. He didn't, and it won him a great deal of respect from his players.

Although not nearly as public, I have experienced my own share of disappointments and defeats. I appreciate how tempting it is to assign blame, to magnify the mistakes of others while downplaying one's personal involvement. However, when a team experiences defeat and morale is low, it's no time for excuses. It's time for leadership. When the economy is sinking and people are afraid of losing their jobs, they need a leader who is willing to provide creative solutions, instead of looking for the easy way out. When team members make mistakes, they need a leader who is willing to provide an honest assessment of the situation and to look for ways to move forward, instead of assigning blame.

I want our team members to be compassionate, creative, hardworking people who are willing to pull themselves up by their bootstraps when the going gets tough. And, if those are the sort of people I want on the team, then I have to be that sort of

Downtown Cedar Rapids during the flood of 2008

person myself. I have to be the guy I want to hire. Hayden has taught me so much about expecting as much, or more, from myself than I do from my team. A leader has to lead the way.

The Midwestern floods of 2008, one of the worst U.S. disasters to date, hit our town of Cedar Rapids, Iowa, hard. Even though it is impossible to quantify the total damage, our local newspaper estimated that 6,000 homes were lost or damaged, and that losses to private business and industry totaled more than $800 million in our county alone.[2] Many of our employees

Brandon, Paige, Deanna, and Tom

and associates were affected by the flooding and experienced unthinkable inconvenience and loss.

In an effort to help, we started the Berthel Fisher 2008 Flood Relief Fund with a deposit of $100,000. It was not meant to be the totality of the fund, but a start. We wanted to lead the way and to encourage others to follow suit. Almost instantly, we began receiving a significant number of calls and e-mails from our representatives across the country, wanting to donate to the fund and asking what else they could do to help. I was so proud of our team. I was proud of their selflessness and their willingness to give of themselves and of their personal resources to help others.

These fundamental leadership strategies will also enhance family productivity and closeness. As with business and politics, families are faced with ups and downs and uncertain futures. From tragedies to celebrations, families often get caught up in the extremes and need a leader to help steady the ship. Family members help us through crises and join us in celebrating victories.

In a busy world, with Twitter, text messaging, and Facebook, it can seem virtually impossible to achieve face-to-face "locker-room time" with family. Consider the most important members of your family team. How have you been treating them? When we fail, we must use the family locker room to regroup, reestablish the game plan, and remind everyone of the family goals. It always pays off. Love and determination help to create strong families and become a leader's greatest assets. Sometimes, especially for guys, it is difficult to communicate and to have these locker-room moments with family, but if we take some of our leadership methods home, we might just discover a greater sense of family camaraderie and synergy. A strong, healthy, winning family may be closer than you think.

Through many years and many ups and downs, I have tried to keep the focus on people, not dollars. Following the example of leaders like H. L. Hunt and Hayden Fry, I have not forgotten my humble beginnings. I keep things as simple as possible, and I do my best to lead by example. As a result, I am continually blessed with a team of people who demonstrates collective buy-in. Not only do they care genuinely about one another and the leadership of the company, but they also work hard every day, regardless of the obstacles in front of them, to create a shared success story that we can all be proud of. That is something money simply cannot buy.

POSTGAME WITH COACH FRY

Modeling the way

I've had so many great leaders in my life who have taught me how to live and who have modeled the way for me. To start at the beginning, I'd have to go back seventy-some years and start with my own father. He was very tough on me, and held me to a very high standard, but he taught me the value of discipline and the importance of having convictions worth fighting for.

During my teen years, my black buddies modeled the way for me by showing me how to deal with rejection and injustice. If they had to sit in the back of the bus, I sat in the back of the bus with them. If they had to sit in the balcony of the theater, I sat up there with them. I saw them endure so many things that were unfair and even mean, yet they pressed on, and many excelled in spite of (or maybe because of) the adversity they faced. Knowing them and being friends with them encouraged and prepared me for the Jerry LeVias years.

For better or worse, I think inadvertent role-modeling speaks much louder than intentional good deeds. We have to be careful. I really don't think my father, or high school coaches, or my friends woke up in the morning with the goal of showing me how to live. They just lived and let me watch.

People watch us every day, whether we know it or not, and our influence reaches farther than we may ever realize. For instance, I never realized the impact I had on Tom until

Tom and Hayden

I read the pages of this book. I love Tom, but I've never rolled out of bed in the morning with the goal of inspiring him. Of course, it's a great honor to know now that our talks and the time we've spent together have made a difference in his life. The reason they have, though, is because he is always paying attention. He asks a lot of questions, and, having been a football coach for forty-seven years, the only way I know to answer him is with stories about football. What is your story? What have you learned that might inspire someone else?

As a coach, you're always on the line. Your guys may or may not function on a given day, but the buck stops with you. It is the coach's responsibility to make the tough calls and to do what needs to be done, even if it's not popular. Passing the buck never made anyone a great role model.

We've had some great leaders in this country who have been handed huge responsibilities, and certainly one of the most daunting tasks has been the handling of our nation's response to 9/11. As is the case with most Americans, the images of that day are forever carved in my mind. I was sitting on the back porch of our home on Iowa's Coralville Reservoir when news of the first plane crashing into the World Trade Center came across our television screen. I ran inside and called Shirley, my wife, to come to the TV. We both stood in utter shock as we witnessed the second plane crash into the second tower. I couldn't believe what we were seeing.

As a coach, I've lost my share of football games, but lives were never at stake. Every time I've lost a game, I've had to answer the hard questions about what went wrong and how I planned to fix it. All I could think of, as Shirley and I stood and watched the horrors of that day unfold, was about the responsibility just handed to President Bush. What on earth was he going to do? What type of message was he going to send out to his team? To America? How was he going to lead his Cabinet and military to react to this insanity? What kind of game plan would they be able to come up with to effectively lead this broken nation? I was really into the leadership aspect of it.

Nearly everyone in the country could personally identify with the tragedy in one way or another, and we were all depending on our leaders to provide comfort and protection.

George H. W. Bush has been a friend of mine for years, and he asked me to introduce his son, President George W. Bush, at an event in Iowa, not long after the tragedy of 9/11. Prior to the event, I took the opportunity to offer some encouragement. "Mr. President," I said, "I coached football for forty-seven years, and to my knowledge, I never had a coach or players make a mistake on purpose. I feel the same way about you and your Cabinet. You have experts and generals advising you on what to do, just like I had coaches advising me. You have to make decisions based on their advice and your own gut instinct. To me, Mr. President, you didn't make any bad decisions. You were protecting America."

I first became acquainted with George H. W. Bush when he came to watch Odessa win the state football championship in Austin, Texas, against Thomas Jefferson San Antonio. Right after the game he tapped me on the shoulder and said, "Hayden, I want to congratulate you on the championship. I've watched your last three games and I'm really impressed. I just moved to Odessa to take a job with an oil field supply company, and my wife, Barbara, is still back up in the Northeast. We're looking for a place to rent in Odessa. Do you happen to know of one?"

It just so happened that my girlfriend's parents had recently renovated their garage into an apartment. I had no idea who George Bush was at the time, but I told him about the apartment and he rented it when he returned to Odessa. He and Barbara lived there for six months before moving 20 miles to

Midland, Texas. History books say that George W. was born in Midland, but there are a whole lot of folks in West Texas that know he was conceived in Odessa.

George W. heard me tell that story from time to time, and he liked it so much that he asked me to tell it to his Cabinet prior to the opening ceremonies of the 2002 Winter Olympics Games in Salt Lake City. Well, the whole bunch—Condoleezza Rice, Colin Powell, John Ashcroft—they all broke up laughing. As soon as I'd finished the story, George W. walked up to me with a real grim face and put his hands on my shoulders. I'm thinking something's terribly wrong, and ask, "Mr. President, did I say something wrong?"

He looked me square in the eye and with a very sincere and solemn voice said, "Coach, I just want you to know—this is the first time my Cabinet has had the opportunity to laugh since I took office." He and Laura are the greatest people, and our nation drew a lot of strength from them during some tough days.

6

THE PSYCHOLOGY OF TEAM

Cultivating a productive culture

THROUGHOUT THE HISTORY of television, sitcoms have captured and romanticized the culture of family in the workplace. We all felt like part of the fictional Boston bar, Cheers, "where everybody knows your name, and they're always glad you came." We could count on Sam, Diane, Norm, and all the regulars to be there every week, laughing together, fighting together, and helping one another face life's problems.

We celebrated when our longtime friends at the M*A*S*H unit in Korea prepared to return home. The family of Hawkeye Pierce and his cronies entered our hearts and homes for more than a decade, and we were captivated by the way they laughed together, cried together, feared together, hoped together, and, of course, annoyed one another.

More recently, we've been entertained by *The Office* crew of Dunder Mifflin Paper Company in Scranton, Pennsylvania. Their childish pranks and quirky management practices make us laugh and, even though (or maybe because) they are so dysfunctional, we've come to see them as a family.

These television shows are successful because they capture an essence of family that we can relate to, and they help us find humor in stressful human relationships. However, in real life, bar tabs need to be paid, surgeries need to be performed, and orders need to be processed.

Coming to work with the sole agenda of having fun, engaging in endless conversations about life, and becoming completely absorbed in one another's personal drama is not the sort of family culture that creates a successful team. Fun? Maybe. Interesting? Certainly. Productive? No.

As Charles Sykes points out in his book, *50 Rules Kids Won't Learn in School,* television is not real life. "Your life is not a sitcom," he tells us. "Your problems will not all be solved in 30 minutes, minus time for commercials. In real life, people actually have to leave the coffee shop to go to jobs."

In real life, M*A*S*H units (Mobile Army Surgical Hospitals) are the hope of wounded soldiers. They treat the injuries of war, maintain sterilized equipment and medical supplies, and are ready to pack up and relocate at a moment's notice. Companies manufacture and sell products, serve customers, train employees, and have payroll to meet. Restaurants and bars have to pass health inspections, manage inventories, and keep their customers happy. Being successful, whatever the main objective, requires so much more than just fun and friendship.

There is a great distinction between creating a family atmosphere and building a productive family. The first is based on emotion, the second on authentic success. Please don't misunderstand: It is important that we care about one another, and it is important that we have fun together, but it is absolutely vital that we succeed together. And success requires several components that are rarely seen in television sitcoms.

First, as discussed in chapter three, the team must be composed of people who fit the mission of the company. If a productive culture is to be achieved, then the process of assembling team members is the first and most essential component. Hayden evaluated the whole person when recruiting players and coaches (academics, athletic ability, social life, family, etc.) and maintained his position of skeptic when it came to a person's willingness to change. He reasoned that if a particular player was satisfied with low academic achievement in high school, then he was likely to be satisfied with low academic achievement in college. If a player made poor social decisions during high school, then he was likely to continue this pattern in college.

Likewise, if a company wants productive salespeople, then they must hire productive salespeople. If a company wants good communicators with positive attitudes, then they must hire good communicators with positive attitudes. A productive culture can simply not be cultivated if more time is spent reforming, rather than training, team members.

In addition to assembling a team of like-minded members, ultimate authority must be clearly established. There are few quicker ways to frustrate a team and compromise a mission than for leadership to be ambiguous.

Companies that are committed to growth are likely to experience a few bumps in the road with regard to leadership, and our company is no exception. During tough times, I continue to find great wisdom and guidance in Hayden's philosophy of establishing ultimate authority. He has taught me that I must, as the CEO, work as hard as—or harder than—my team and carry out my role with decisiveness and humility. Hayden never used his position of authority as a power trip. Instead, he embraced it with an attitude of personal responsibility. "If my ship went down, I wanted to be the guy that put the hole in it," he says.

As head coach, Hayden called all of his team's plays, believing that "the head coach needs to be the head coach." He spent countless hours studying the game, making sure he was well educated about what was needed in order to win. Calling the plays forced Hayden to be an informed leader and it eliminated ambiguity. Everyone on the team knew he worked hard to make winning decisions on their behalf, taking into account their input. When things didn't go as planned, his team was confident that Coach would accept full responsibility for game decisions, shielding them from scrutiny by media and fans.

His players and assistant coaches understood their roles, on and off the field. They appreciated and respected Hayden's commitment to work harder than anyone else on the team and, as a result, his authority was energizing rather than oppressive. His team didn't resent submitting to his authority because they wholeheartedly believed that Hayden acted in the best interest of the team, not himself.

We have about half a dozen executive positions at our company, which definitely leaves room for ambiguity within

Photo Credit: UIowa Photo Service

Hayden and Penn State Coach Joe Paterno

the company's leadership structure. If any of our executives were to work at building his/her own camp, communicating goals and expectations different from my or the company's own, there would be immediate unrest among our team. This doesn't mean we don't have frequent open discussions among the executive team, expressing differing points of view. But, when the decision is made and differences are settled, a united front of ultimate authority must be presented.

During an intense battle scene in the submarine movie *U-571*, the dwindling American crew appears shaken and fearful. In the midst of German attacks, they rapidly lose confidence and hope, and it is up to their newly appointed commanding officer to get his team refocused and ready to fight. A bit shaken himself, and unsure of how to proceed, a fellow officer sharply reminds the CO, "You're the skipper now, and the skipper always knows what to do whether he does or not."[1] A team needs their leader to lead with confidence, especially during tough times.

When team members lack clarity with regard to leadership, productivity begins to crumble. When leaders use positions of authority to intimidate or degrade team members, the collective team spirit is crushed. On the other hand, when ultimate authority is clearly defined and humbly executed, team members thrive and everybody wins.

Much of the challenge in establishing ultimate authority and creating a productive culture hinges on the way team members communicate with one another. Does each member feel valued? Are expectations clear? Is it safe to express ideas? Are missteps viewed as opportunities to learn, or as failures? Honest communication builds trust, and trust is fundamental to team morale.

The 1986 Rose Bowl ended in a hard loss for the Hawkeyes. Iowa closed the regular season with a record of 10–1, holding on to first place for several weeks before a late-season upset to number-eight Ohio State. Even though the Hawkeyes slipped to number three in the Coaches' Poll, they claimed the Big Ten title for just the second time in twenty-seven years. Going on to win the Rose Bowl, which they were favored to do, may have clinched the Hawkeyes' hope of bringing home a national championship.

Game day in Pasadena began foggy and overcast, which was fitting for the disappointment to follow. Not only was quarterback Chuck Long sacked four times, but running back Ronnie Harmon also fumbled the ball four times and dropped a sure

Photo Credit: UIowa Photo Service

Ronnie Harmon

touchdown pass in the end zone late in the game. It wasn't the finale they had envisioned as they stepped off the bus at the Rose Bowl. Instead of taking home a national title, the Hawkeyes took home memories of mistakes, even controversy.

It is in these times that honest communication builds unshakable trust and reminds the team that they will live to win another day. When a team wins, Hayden insists that they win as a team. When they lose, he insists that they lose as a team. He has never been interested in hearing excuses. He is interested in conducting an honest evaluation of why the *team* lost, and how they plan to fix it.

When controversy arose over Harmon's fumbles, Hayden resisted the opportunity to point fingers. He stood by his team and projected a united front. "Nobody fumbles the ball on purpose," Hayden told reporters. "UCLA hit hard and knocked the ball loose. That's it."

This doesn't mean that everyone was patted on the back or given unwarranted praise. A hard look and many hours of assessment were dedicated to identifying mistakes that were made before and during the game. Together, the coaches and players identified the problems and proposed solutions. Together, they prepared to win again.

Hayden has never been accused of being soft, and he has chewed on his share of reporters, but when it came to his coaches and players—win or lose—they were in it together, and everyone did what it took to help the team succeed. You see, when Coach Fry and his team stepped off the bus that day in Pasadena, they stepped off as a team. When they returned to the bus, after a gut-wrenching and controversial loss, they returned as a team.

Through honest evaluation and communication, trust is established. When team members truly trust one another, they treat each other with respect, share the task of identifying obstacles and overcoming mistakes, and work hard to achieve collective success.

Finally, part of cultivating a productive culture is having fun together. Teams want to have fun together and they are more successful when they do. Celebrating success is fun. Being appreciated is fun. Engaging in healthy competition is fun. Playing together is fun.

In fact, fun is a value at Berthel Fisher. It is part of our everyday culture and one of the primary objectives for our annual convention. I'm not talking about clowns and confetti. I'm talking about celebrating the success and dreams of the Berthel Fisher team. We make time to publicly recognize outstanding performances. We announce the always-exotic destination of our next President's Club Conference and encourage *every* team member to catch the vision of joining us there. We make it a family affair by including spouses in the celebration, and we've even been known to wear cowboy hats and do a little two-stepping on the dance floor.

Winning is fun, and Hayden made fun part of his game-day preparation as well. Every now and then, when practices were plagued with missed tackles and dropped balls, he'd call everything to a halt and gather the whole team in the middle of the

Hayden and Shirley Fry at Berthel's 2008 Annual Convention

Hawkeye swarm

field. "We'd have a sing-along right there and then," Hayden says. "I'd get a couple of the team comedians up front to tell a joke or two until everybody was laughing and hollerin'. We lightened up their mental attitudes and it never failed. As soon as we broke up the party, every guy would get back to work and stop making mistakes. You can't take yourselves too seriously."

Having earned a degree in psychology, Hayden is a master at cultivating a productive culture, and I've learned so much from him about team-building. Everything Hayden did behind the scenes to create a productive culture, from recruiting the right people to establishing ultimate authority and honest communication, was reflected on the field in something called "The Swarm."

Every game day, regardless of the opponent or the predictions of pundits, the Hawkeyes take the field holding hands in one big, intimidating swarm. It was, and still is, a public display of the togetherness and selflessness that is cultivated in the locker room and on the practice field. The players may be scared to death on the inside, but the other team never knows it. They're a family. And they're there to win the game together.

POSTGAME WITH COACH FRY

The psychology of team

I love the psychology involved in building a successful team. As Tom writes in this chapter, it doesn't happen by accident. It has to be an intentional mind-set, and you have to take a genuine interest in each player, individually. If every one of my players didn't feel like a valuable, contributing member of the team, then we would never win. It doesn't matter if a guy plays every quarter of the ball game or supports his team from the sidelines—he has to completely believe that his role is an essential piece of the puzzle. And it was my job, as the leader, to build a unified team.

I got interested in what makes people tick when I was still in high school. My buddies and I used to go downtown and sit on the fenders of cars, just killing time. We'd watch people walk down the street and guess what sort of profession they were in, how old they were, what sort of religion they practiced, and so on. Once we'd sized someone up, one of us would run down the street and ask the person questions to see how close we were at guessing things correctly. I got pretty good at figuring people out, and that's when I first realized how interested I was in studying human behavior.

Of course, working in the oil fields, I just assumed I'd major in geology or some other related area in college. It wasn't until later that I decided to major in psychology, and I've really enjoyed learning why people think the way they do, what motivates them, what turns them on and off. It ended up being a great benefit to me in coaching.

As I learned more and more about people, I began to understand that we take more risks and work harder when we're confident in the brainpower and loyalty of our leader. I had success in coaching because I tried to work harder and study more than anyone else on the team, and it created a sense of security. You see, I'm not that smart, but I pay attention.

I played quarterback in junior high, high school, college, and then for the Marine Corps, so I have always been very motivated to study defensive strategies. Educating myself on the defensive tendencies of my opponents helped me to anticipate the best offensive-play calls. And it was this knowledge that gave

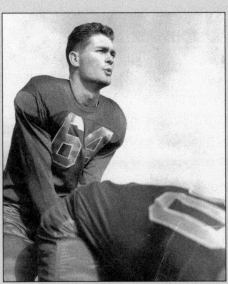

me the confidence to call all the plays as a head coach. Not only did it give me a better handle on the game, but it also put me in a position to take the brunt of any criticism.

Every time I called a play at Kinnick Stadium that didn't work as planned, there was an old Iowa farmer in the stands who was

John Hayden Fry, quarterback,
Baylor University

happy to give me the credit. He was there for every game, about twenty rows behind my bench, wearing bib overalls and a straw hat, about six-foot-four and 275 pounds. "Fry," he'd yell, with his hands cupped around his mouth, "you dummy!" Every time he yelled it, I'd turn around and stare at him, and think to myself: *Now, here's a guy who's probably never worn a jockstrap in his life, telling me how to call the game.*

No player wants to fumble the ball. No quarterback sets out to have his pass intercepted. And no coach wants to call a bad play. But life is tough and sometimes things go wrong. There are so many variables in coaching—administration, team politics, media, fans—and people are standing in line to second-guess every decision a coach makes. My team had to know that I supported them, no matter what. They had to trust my preparedness and my intentions. In turn, I protected

Photo Credit: UIowa Photo Service

my players and coaches by accepting full responsibility for foul-ups.

When sportscasters wanted access to one of our players, in order to hammer him on a mistake, we just didn't provide the access. We had a set time, every Tuesday afternoon, for media interviews. Otherwise, the players were off limits. I was determined to protect our team from media hype. Making some players out to be heroes, while completely ignoring others, is a perfect way to destroy team morale and to create divisions within the team.

Another key ingredient to any success I experienced was to create trust among our coaching staff. We started every day with a staff meeting, in which we talked extensively and honestly about our organization, planned our practice schedule, talked about recruiting, and studied our opponents' films. We were all in it together. We prepared as a team, we played as a team, and we presented a united front to the players, win or lose. No one was allowed to take all the credit or assume all the blame.

If you haven't figured it out yet, I despise blame games. There's nothing productive about them. In fact, they're nothing but a waste of breath, and this is why I got along so well with the officials. They are there to keep an eye on the game and to call it the way they see it. Sometimes I saw things differently, but if the official made a mistake, I had to remind myself and my team that it wasn't on purpose. In my head I might be thinking, "That son of a gun—why'd he do that?"

Photo Credit: UIowa Photo Service

But I never said anything out loud. We had some bad calls go against us, but we benefited from some, too. It all has a way of evening out.

It's no secret that I love winning, but I had to learn to have fun with my teams in order to create a winning culture. When I first became a head coach, I was pretty uptight and hesitant to do things that would lighten things up when the boys fouled up. That was something I had to learn. Eventually, I discovered the power in having an impromptu sing-along in the middle of a tough practice, or having the guys tell a few jokes.

Off the field, we built team chemistry by encouraging the guys to spend time together having fun, within the rules that had been established. This was something that was very hard for Jerry LeVias. He sat in his dorm room alone for two years before anybody asked him to do anything socially. It wasn't until he proved himself and we started winning that his teammates were willing to take the risk. We were charting new waters with Jerry, and it was a very difficult time for everyone.

Playing a sport teaches such great life lessons. There's discipline, organization, hard work, respect, teamwork, playing by the rules. Every time you do something wrong, there's a guy in a striped shirt who throws a flag. That's life. Every boy and girl should be encouraged to get involved in sports. It's not about scholarships or glory, but about learning. You have to maintain a certain academic average to participate. You can't drink or smoke. You have to pay attention to nutrition and stay in good physical shape. As a bonus, you experience the joy of playing the game and develop lifelong friendships. And it all carries over to adulthood.

There are few things more rewarding than being part of a motivated, cohesive team. When adversity comes, you don't have to face it alone. When victories come, there are always people to share the experience. It's all about psychology, and every leader simply has to go the extra mile to teach and model the values and habits of a productive culture. Win together, lose together. No exceptions.

7

KNOW WHERE YOU ARE ON THE FIELD

Establishing a game plan

AFTER RETURNING A punt, the offense is set on their own 23-yard line, 77 yards from the goal. Systematically, the quarterback passes the ball down the field. Play after play, the wide receivers and tight ends create room for middle crossing routes. Down after down, the inside receiver runs a deep route up the middle, taking the safety with him and allowing the outside receiver to get open underneath. All the way down the field, they make easy receptions and have room to run. Before the defense figures out how to stop the passing game, it's first and goal.

The drive down the field is flawless. The passing game is working. Now, in the red zone, the offense changes everything and throws something unexpected at the defense. The

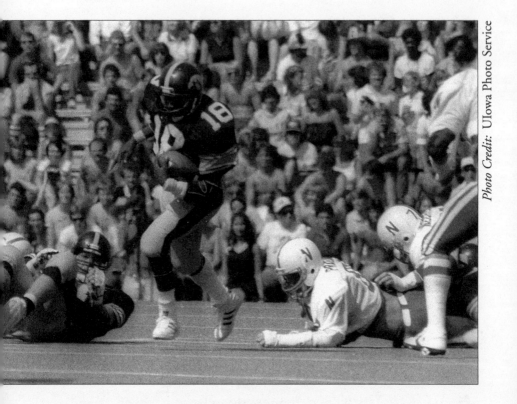

quarterback calls a running play, attempting to punch the ball up the middle and into the end zone. Three times they go for the run. Three times the defense holds them back. No touchdown.

On the field and off the field, sometimes lessons are hard-learned, and the unexpected can lead to unforgettable results. When Hayden was nine years old, growing up in Odessa, Texas, he had to do morning chores every day before breakfast. One of his chores was to milk the cows. On his way to the barn, Hayden would grab two pails (one to sit on, one to fill) and waste no time getting to work. One winter morning, after milking their old black-and-white cow, he turned to set the pail of milk up on the back porch. Just as he did, he caught a glimpse of his dad leaning against the barn door watching him. "You didn't get all of the milk, son," his dad announced.

"Yes, sir, I did," Hayden replied, his breath turning white in the cold morning air. Without a word, his dad grabbed the half-full pail, headed toward the black-and-white cow, and started squeezing. Before Hayden could come up with a proper defense, the bucket was full.

"Come with me, son," his dad grumbled as he took Hayden by the ear and led him out the back door of the barn, just out of his mother's sight. Clutching a horse whip, his dad said, "Son, bend over. I want you to remember this for the rest of your life." *Whawp.* The sting of the leather made Hayden straighten his back and bite his lip to keep from crying. *Whawp.*

Still fighting back tears, Hayden looked up at his dad just in time to interrupt the next *whawp,* asking, "Daddy, what is it that you want me to remember?"

"Son," his dad said, "if you've got something good going for you, squeeze it till it's dry."

It should be no surprise that Hayden still remembers the lesson he learned that morning, and, as a result, he has told me more than once, "You can bet your bottom dollar, if a play gets you to the goal line, it'll get you across the goal line."

I've watched so many football games that tell the same story that starts this chapter. A team moves the football the entire length of the field, gets to the 10-yard line, and forgets how they got there. It doesn't mean trick plays and offensive adjustments are a bad idea. Sometimes it's necessary to change things up a bit, but sometimes teams need to follow Mr. Fry's advice and "squeeze it till it's dry"—sticking with the plays that got them to the goal line in the first place.

In business, as in football, a well-managed playbook is the difference between victory and defeat. You have to know where you're at on the field and know, with confidence, what it's going to take to get across the goal line. When do you go with your bread-and-butter play? When do you take a flier and call a trick play? When do you punt on third down? Ask ten winning football coaches and you'll get ten different answers, but there will be one thing in common: a clear goal, a game plan to get there, and a lot of hard work.

The day H. L. Hunt shared his peanut-butter-and-jelly sandwich with Hayden, he told him that his recipe for success had been to make up his mind what he wanted (establishing a clear goal), to figure out a way to do it (developing a game plan), and then to simply do it (working hard).

During the fuel shortage of 1946, Hunt supplied 85 percent of the natural gas piped into the eastern states and had become the largest independent oil producer in the United States. He was also a successful real estate investor, one of the largest pecan growers in the country, and was involved in the production of a variety of consumer products, including canned goods, health products, and cosmetics. By the time of his death in 1974, Mr. Hunt was worth nearly $3 billion and making a million dollars a week.[1]

Business success is obviously something H. L. Hunt mastered, and he did so by following a very simple plan: Establish a clear goal, develop a game plan, and work . . . work . . . work. He didn't waste time dreaming about success—he chased it.

Clear goals and well-defined game plans provide clarity in the midst of the daily grind. When new opportunities come along or mistakes are made, the game plan becomes an essential decision-making tool to keep you on the right track. It keeps you focused and helps you do what Hayden calls "scouting your own team." Scouting your own team means educating yourself and being honest about all of the variables involved. It gives you a foundation for decision-making and helps you determine which plays will get you across the goal line.

Football coaches must scout positions, personnel, schedules, opponents, injuries, and the weather on game day, and they must be prepared for the unexpected. A well-defined game plan is the only credible resource for accurately understanding and managing variables. What are our strengths? What are our weaknesses? Does the proposed change fit within our game plan? Great opportunities arise that aren't necessarily great fits for every team. Unless you are completely honest with yourself and have a solid grasp of the situation, decisions can become emotional instead of rational.

Tom Landry's Cowboys had nine different ways to run around the end. It was beautiful. But even though he had the chance, Hayden never borrowed Coach Landry's Dallas playbook. Because Hayden scouted his own team and had a well-defined game plan, he knew he didn't have the personnel to execute Landry's plays and he wasn't sure he could coach them. They were great plays, winning plays, but they weren't the right plays for Hayden's team.

Several years ago, I was asked to invest in a fish farm that was going to "feed the world." Great opportunity. Noble opportunity.

Right? As we boarded the private plane that would fly us to the fish farm, our executive team was optimistic. The idea intrigued us, and we went with an open mind. We also went with a set of clearly defined criteria that the project would have to meet in order to fit within our existing game plan. So, away we flew to sunny California.

The sales pitch during the flight was convincing. The new technology used for the fish tanks would virtually eliminate the need for offshore fishing and was sure to make our clients millions. As we approached the landing site, we observed several underground silos, topped with enormous white lids. The lids, we learned, were part of a state-of-the-art temperature-control system which delivered a high degree of quality and cost control.

As we exited the plane and walked to one of the silos, our interest was piqued; I was excited to get a closer look. Slowly, the lid was lifted off the giant pool to reveal the little critters that could make us millions. Much to our surprise, and our enterpriser's dismay, there had been a temperature malfunction and we were greeted by hundreds of dead fish floating at the top of the pool. Needless to say, we opted for steak at dinner that night.

This story isn't meant to devalue the fish-farm idea. Once the bugs had been worked out, it may indeed have developed into the million-dollar opportunity we had hoped for. The point, though, is that we protected ourselves from financial loss because we were purposeful in researching the opportunity. Rather than making an emotional decision based on hearsay, we sought the facts. Due diligence is not an exact science, but it does help you avoid some of the bad deals.

Another investment opportunity that came our way involved a company that manufactured french-fry dispensing machines.

This, unlike the fish farm, was a business that had received a considerable amount of capital to get off the ground and was already experiencing success. Our company was contacted and asked to consider a financial investment that would take the french-fry company to the next level. If we decided to invest, machines would be installed all over the world and special effort would be made to infiltrate college dormitories nationwide. Who better to plug quarters into a machine for a hot bag of greasy, salty fries than college students? It sounded reasonable to us.

BFC executive staff: Tom Berthel, Julie Driscoll, and Dwight Wheelan, 1993

Again, our executive team ventured across the country to scout the opportunity. There we stood, in front of a french-fry machine, waiting with great anticipation. Our tour guide popped a few coins into the machine and soon, one by one, french fries were slowly dropped into the bag below. Cool. Ron Brendengen looked at me curiously, walked to the side of the machine, and peered around the back. "Is there a guy in there?" he asked with a smile. "That could get expensive."

As with every opportunity to come our way, we weighed the french-fry investment against our existing goals and considered how it would impact our current game plan. We scouted the situation thoroughly. Even though it was an intriguing concept, the conclusion was that it just wasn't a good fit for us, and we passed.

Several months later, I received a phone call offering a "great opportunity" to invest in a company that manufactured french-fry-dispensing machines. It was selling at the "bargain price" of ten cents on the dollar. That's why you game-plan. Had we allowed ourselves to be persuaded by the "cool factor" instead of relying on our game plan, we would have made a bad business decision and experienced significant financial loss.

Ironically, our industry is often hit with french-fry machines and dead fish. Great fortunes have been made and lost on entrepreneurial ideas. Many investors insist on chasing the big win only to end up in the hole. Innovation and new company start-ups often create wealthy investors, so it makes sense that investors try to get in on the ground floor of things. Initial Public Offerings (IPOs) and other private placements also add to the investment frenzy. The best way to handle such opportunities is to play them smart.

If you can't afford to lose, don't play. Know exactly where you're at on the financial field of play, and don't count on the Hail Mary pass to save you. If the scoreboard tells you that you can't afford to lose the ball, go with a short pass. Sometimes slow and steady gets to the finish line first. If you do decide to go deep, keep an extra blocker in. The best way to protect is to prepare for the downside, and to understand that you may have to punt sometimes on third down to avoid losing the ball.

Over the years, I have followed Hayden's advice to capitalize on plays that work and eliminate plays that don't. It sounds simple, but a lot of companies neglect to do it. There are CEOs all over the world fiddling with things they can't handle. The variables aren't right to execute a particular idea, but they press

Tom Berthel, 1976

forward anyway. They can't identify the problem because they aren't consulting a preset plan, and they end up becoming their own worst opponent. They end up beating themselves.

There is no shame in admitting weakness. Shame comes only when we're unwilling to be honest with ourselves and our team, and we end up in the tank.

When I was just starting out in business, I was invited to join a morning coffee club. It was fun at first. It gave me a chance to visit with other business-minded people and to bounce ideas around. Soon, I realized that the topics of conversation were circuitous. Every week we "talked around the world and back," without accomplishing anything. The conversations were interesting, but it was all talk and no action. Good ideas and brilliant solutions were shared consistently, but no action plan was ever established. I soon realized, however interesting the meeting was, that it was not helping me achieve my personal goals, and that it was, instead, taking valuable time away from my game plan. Once I figured out that it wasn't just the coffee elevating my blood pressure, I dismissed myself from the group.

The morning coffee club gave me a glimpse of life without a plan. It was good ideas and viable solutions spinning endlessly in unproductive circles. Few people are ever really lucky. Luck is almost always the result of hard work and a purposeful direction. It is the "residue of design," as former Brooklyn Dodgers General Manager Branch Rickey famously said. Game plans are fallible, of course, but they provide a sense of purpose and direction. They provide security and spur productivity. Unfortunately, many entrepreneurs fail to develop or stick to a good game plan or to rework their plan when it proves ineffective.

Hayden would never have dreamed of stepping onto a football field on game day without a precise plan of action, and a complete understanding of all the variables. He knew that his offense would take more risks when playing closer to midfield. He knew they would play conservatively if trapped near their own goal line. His team knew never to act like they'd scored a touchdown unless they actually did. And, most important, he knew that losing a single game did not change the ultimate goal of becoming a winner.

Opportunities are everywhere and ideas are endless. Each of us has twenty-four hours in a day, seven days a week, and fifty-two weeks a year to chase our dreams. We must understand our own field position and act accordingly. It's not a matter of how much time or ambition we have; it's a matter of how we use our time and how we focus our ambition. Time and focus are what determine whether our story will be one of success, mediocrity, or failure. How is your story going to end?

POSTGAME WITH COACH FRY

Know where you are on the field

The Texas Rangers are a rich part of the history and legends of the Old West, and my dad's daddy was one of them. Captain Bill McDonald, a fellow Texas Ranger, once said, "No man in the wrong can stand up against a fellow that's in the right and keep on a-comin'." The Rangers were tough men, living in tough days, and my granddaddy was no exception. Standing six-foot-three, he never learned to write his name. In fact, he once sold a horse for five dollars and when he was asked to sign the receipt, Granddad just marked the spot with an X. He was tough as nails till the day he died, at age eighty-six, and he raised my daddy to work hard and live well.

In turn, my dad learned to be tough. He was tough on me and expected a great deal from me. Even so, I never disliked him for it because he was very good at getting me to understand exactly what he wanted me to learn. I didn't always get it at the time, but there was so much truth in the things my dad said. He really made a great impression on me (or should I say, the horse whip did), and I greatly admired him for it. Sadly, he died of a massive heart attack at the age of fifty-three, so our years together were cut too short.

I would never have become the coach I was without the discipline and lessons I learned from my dad. By the time I began coaching, I understood completely that anything worth doing is worth doing well, and that you can never work too hard. I knew that if I didn't do my homework in preparing a solid game plan for my team, making tough decisions and establishing the highest expectations for execution, we weren't going to win. It's as simple as that. I never thought of it as being mean or tough. My guys wanted to win as much as I did, so they listened to me and they worked hard to carry out our plan.

John Hayden Fry, Sr., Hayden's father

There are so many things that go into developing a solid game plan. We had to scout ourselves on a regular basis. We had to overcome losses by analyzing mistakes and correcting them. If we tried something and it didn't work, we didn't keep doing it over and over. We simply gave it up and moved on. We had to learn how to respond to winning. We had to know every detail about our opponents and their tendencies. We had to exercise restraint, learning that we didn't have to try everything that made sense. Just like I learned from H. L. Hunt, we had to build on what worked and keep it simple.

As the head coach, it was my job to communicate the game plan and to teach the coaches and players how to execute it. If a player didn't know exactly what to do, then I took full

Photo Credit: UIowa Photo Service

Coaching All-American quarterback Chuck Long

responsibility. We spent hours making sure our guys knew exactly how to hold the ball, catch the ball, make the tackle, and run the plays. When leaders take full responsibility for implementing the game plan, it creates a culture of trust.

In my younger days, when one of my coaches called a failed play from the press box, I called up and said, "Coach, you're fired. You're done." It was reported to me later that the poor guy took his headset off, looked around at the other coaches in the box, and said with a stunned voice, "He just fired me." It's not something I'm proud of, but I learned a great deal from it. You just can't do that. Nobody makes a bad call on purpose. Every mistake is an appeal for more instruction.

Photo Credit: UIowa Photo Service

If I ever put my hands on a player, it wasn't to chew him out or shame him. It may have looked that way to the television cameras, but I was always looking for ways to call him to a higher level of performance—to build him up. All it took with Chuck Long, my All-American quarterback, was to grab hold of his shoulder pads, find his eyes through the face mask, and say, "Chuck, you're better than that." It worked.

The biggest mistakes any leader can make, when creating and carrying out a game plan, is to ignore the people he employs and to shame them for their mistakes. First, you have to listen to the advice and suggestions of your team. If you don't listen to them, they won't listen to you. Second, you have to take responsibility for final decisions. Win as a team, lose as a team. Of course, this can be one of the most difficult things for a leader to do, and it takes a great deal of restraint at times, but it is possible—and most productive—to correct mistakes without demoralizing anyone.

Coming up with a successful game plan is one of my favorite things about coaching. There are few things more rewarding than winning a big game after spending hours and hours analyzing previous mistakes, studying the opponent, developing new plays, improving existing plays, and deciding which plays need to be eliminated from the playbook. And I will never forget the feeling of seeing the smiles on the faces of a bunch of dirty, sweaty guys who worked their hearts out all week, studying and executing a game plan, which ultimately led to victory.

8

THE ART OF ANTICIPATION

Lessons from an unsinkable ship

THE RMS TITANIC was thought to be unsinkable. The price tag for her construction was $7 million, which would be more than $400 million today. A first-class parlor suite ticket could be purchased for $4,350, which is as much as it would have cost to buy five Model T Fords that same year, 1912.[1]

The *Titanic* measured nearly 300 yards from stem to stern, as long as three football fields placed end to end. She was a floating palace of luxury for the 2,227 people who came aboard, bound for New York on April 10, 1912. She boasted one of the first heated saltwater swimming pools aboard a ship, a Turkish bath full of teakwood, formal dining rooms with the finest china, state-of-the-art wireless radios, and steam-powered generators that allowed passengers to use electric lamps and heaters in their cabins, a luxury few of them enjoyed even in their own homes.[2]

Beyond Xs and Os

Perhaps the most important luxuries aboard *Titanic* were her progressive safety features: fifteen bulkheads that could be closed to create watertight compartments in the event of an emergency, more lifeboats than were legally required by the Board of Trade,[3] and "double-bottom" construction in the ship's hull, which provided added stability at sea. These were the sort of innovative safety features that earned her the reputation of being unsinkable.[4]

As the captain, crew, and passengers waved good-bye to Southampton, surrounded by luxury and supported by an unsinkable ship, they anticipated only the best.

Unsinkable ships. Unbeatable teams. Unbreakable banks. We want desperately to believe in fairy tales. But, as the world learned at 2:20 AM, the tragic morning of April 15, 1912, even the most luxurious, unsinkable ships can sink. As the 2007 New England Patriots learned at Super Bowl XLII, unbeatable teams get beat. And, as Bear Stearns learned in March 2008, unbreakable banks go broke. Optimism is a virtue, but simply anticipating the best does not guarantee the best. Hoping for the fairy tale is a start, but we must also recognize the dangers that threaten our dreams and anticipate the unexpected.

As an officer candidate in the U.S. Marine Corps, Hayden learned that psychological training and mental discipline are the first steps in preparing for the unexpected. Part of his training included the extensive process of setting up a Main Line of Resistance (MLR). When threatened by opposing forces, officers are called upon to establish this most-important system of defense consisting of troops, weaponry, and anti-enemy obstacles. When establishing an MLR, no decisions are made

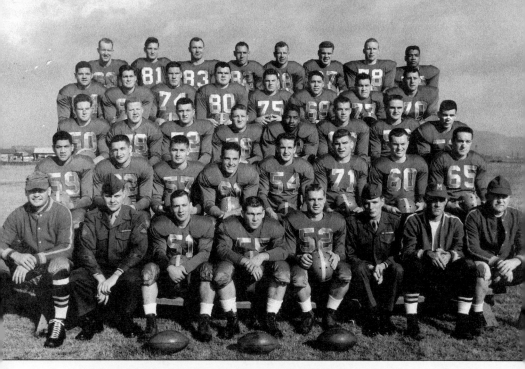

USMC football; Hayden Fry is second from left, fourth row.

or actions taken before a thorough estimate of the situation has been made. Where are we? Where do we need to go? Who is our enemy? What odds do we need to overcome? What supplies are needed? Every positive, negative, and neutral factor must be fully explored and dealt with directly, especially in establishing our best field of fire.

The concept of assessing conditions as a main line of defense against danger became a significant part of Hayden's coaching philosophy and has become part of my leadership practices as well. Making a thorough estimate of the situation protects against deception. When a Marine Corps officer, CEO, football coach, or captain of a ship is fully aware of every positive, negative, and neutral factor at play in a current situation, and then deals with the findings decisively, there is less temptation to rationalize shortcuts or to look for loopholes.

The *Titanic* was a grand ship, and truly warranted the confidence of her passengers and crew, but she was still just a ship made of rivets and steel. The misconception that *Titanic* was unsinkable started with an article published in *Shipbuilder* magazine that claimed the construction of *Titanic*'s watertight doors made her "practically unsinkable."[5]

Titanic's shipbuilders, Harland and Wolff, appear to be the only ones to fully grasp the significance of the word *practically*, and insisted that their customer, the White Star Line, install forty-eight lifeboats to accommodate all passengers in the case of emergency. Their recommendation was rejected. Rather than dealing honestly with the reality of the danger, the White Star Line rationalized a decision to install only twenty lifeboats. They were convinced, along with most of the world, that *Titanic*'s state-of-the-art safety features were sufficient to keep her passengers safe. With each lifeboat consuming 270 square feet of deck space, passenger comfort would surely be compromised by the clutter of twenty-eight additional lifeboats. Besides, *Titanic* was only required to carry sixteen boats according to Board of Trade regulations, so the conclusion, in response to this legal loophole, was that twenty lifeboats were more than enough.[6]

Not dealing with potential problems honestly creates the temptation to rationalize our situation and to look for shortcuts. Had the White Star Line respected the facts of the situation, and prepared for the worst, hundreds of additional lives may have been saved.

The late months of 2008 gave us tragic examples of unbreakable banks and businesses going broke: Washington

Mutual, Bear Stearns, Fannie Mae and Freddie Mac, AIG, Lehman Brothers, Merrill Lynch. Companies and organizations perceived by the general public as unsinkable, sank. Companies that survived the Great Depression were now laid to rest in the history books. Leaders ignored the fundamentals of good business and became deceived by greed. A preventable economic crisis swept through our nation because too many people rationalized the facts and looked for loopholes.

Another threat to the success of our goals and dreams is the danger of becoming overconfident. Arrogance often leads to blind defeat. I'm not talking about healthy pride in accomplishment or the stubborn belief that you can win. I'm talking about believing that you're invincible.

In 1979, Iowa played Indiana at Kinnick Stadium to open the season. Dennis Mosley ran for more than 100 yards and scored four touchdowns in the first half, leading the Hawkeyes into the locker room at halftime with a score of 26–3. The players had every right to take pride in their first-half accomplishment. However, the halftime celebration clearly looked and sounded like it was coming from a team that had already won the game. Hayden knew immediately that they were in trouble. Try as he did to remind his players that there were still thirty minutes of football left to play, he couldn't get them back. They lost their mental edge because they did not know how to handle winning.

As a result, the adjustments Indiana made for the second half of the football game were successful. With a breakdown in Hawkeye pass coverage and a 66-yard touchdown pass, the Hoosiers sealed a 30–26 victory. It was a painful defeat for Hayden's team, but a wonderful learning experience. Although it prevented the Hawkeyes from claiming their first winning season in eighteen years, it taught the players and coaches the danger of overconfidence and the importance of maintaining a solid grasp on reality.

Five years before *Titanic* made her maiden voyage, the would-be Captain E. J. Smith stated:

> *When anyone asks how I can best describe my experience in nearly 40 years at sea, I merely say, uneventful. Of course there have been winter gales, and storms and fog and the like, but in all my experience, I have never been in any accident of any sort worth speaking about. I never saw a wreck and never have been wrecked, nor was I ever in any predicament that threatened to end in disaster of any sort. I cannot imagine any condition which would cause a ship to founder. Modern shipbuilding has gone beyond that.*[7]

Even after word of *Titanic's* disaster began to reach land, executives at the White Star Line held to their confidence (or overconfidence) in *Titanic's* construction. Philip Franklin, vice president of International Mercantile Marine, who controlled the White Star Line, assured the world that passengers were in no real danger. Only after confirming the magnitude of the tragedy did Mr. Franklin issue the following statement to the press:

> *I was confident today when I made the statement that the* Titanic *was unsinkable—that the steamship was safe and that there would be no loss of life. The first definite news to the contrary came in the message this evening from Captain Haddock.*[8]

It is surely this attitude of overconfidence that caused iceberg warnings to be disregarded the night *Titanic* sank. In the weeks following the disaster, *The New York Times* investigated and reported that *Titanic* had received several warnings from a nearby ship. The warnings? Her path was "entangled in a sea of ice skirting an endless field." Sadly, the warnings were ignored and even snubbed by *Titanic's* operator, who replied that he was busy and "did not want to be disturbed." Just ninety minutes after the last warning, an iceberg punctured *Titanic's* hull, and the rest, as they say, is history.[9]

Overconfidence results in denial. The White Star Line denied potential danger when they reduced the number of lifeboats. The captain and crew denied potential danger when they ignored iceberg warnings. But the degree of denial is perhaps best revealed in the response of passengers during the crisis. Belief that *Titanic* was unsinkable was so strong that many refused to board the lifeboats until it was too late. Even from a half-full lifeboat, in the middle of the biting Arctic, passenger Elizabeth Shutes recalled:

> *The first wish on the part of all was to stay near the* Titanic. *We all felt so much safer near the ship. Surely such a vessel could not sink. I thought the danger must be exaggerated, and we could all be taken aboard again.*[10]

The iceberg that sank *Titanic* was mostly underwater and virtually invisible through the calm, dark air of the night. From the first sighting of the iceberg to the first impact was little more than thirty seconds. Two and a half hours later, *Titanic* was bound for her final resting place, 12,000 feet below the ocean.

The danger was predicted. Warnings were given. Still, deception caused overconfidence, overconfidence caused denial, and denial caused fatal error. Whatever the objective, opposition is present and must never be underestimated.

Just as ships face opposition in nature and teams face opposition on the field, businesses face opposition in the marketplace. When tragedy struck Wall Street in 2008, questions flooded our minds: How could this happen, who is to blame, how do we fix it, and how do we stop it from happening again? All valid questions. Our frustration with the economic crisis was fueled by the reality that it may have been prevented if those responsible had dealt with potential dangers honestly and ethically.

Just as Hayden scouted his opponents and developed his game plan accordingly, I am fiercely committed to knowing my opposition and using that knowledge to assist in making responsible decisions on behalf of our brokers and customers. I read everything I can find about the recruiting practices and customer relations of other investment companies. I spend time learning about their strengths, weaknesses, and tendencies so that we can fully understand our own position in the marketplace—good or bad—and understand which routes will keep us most competitive. Our company's departments do what it takes to maintain that edge.

In addition to our competition, we scout appropriate standards and regulations. As Captain Smith and Wall Street executives learned so painfully, regulations and standard operating procedures are not our enemies—unless we choose to ignore them. When the opposition is fully scouted and regulations are respected, there is no excuse for submitting to greed and arrogance. When leaders ignore potential dangers and pursue shortcuts to success, corners get cut, money gets lost, and people get hurt.

Contrary to fairy tales, there are no shortcuts to authentic, lasting success. No fairy godmother waved her magic wand to move the iceberg from *Titanic's* path. No genie in a bottle appeared to undo the damage done on Wall Street. The success of our goals and dreams is dependent on hard work and preparation. It is dependent on anticipating pitfalls and making smart adjustments. It is dependent on expecting the unexpected.

Who would have ever thought the company I started would be bigger than Lehman Brothers and Bear Sterns when it was all said and done? If the U.S. government had not stepped in, we would have overtaken many more. Plugging away one dollar at a time may not be as sexy, but it can still get you there. Calling the right play, at the right time, is very important.

In football, one of a team's greatest assets is the ability to anticipate an opponent's next move. Are they going to run or throw? If they blitz, what areas of weakness can we take advantage of? Larry Station, Hayden's All-American middle linebacker in the early to mid-1980s, was amazing at anticipating plays. In the last minutes of the 1985 Iowa-Michigan game, Iowa trailed by one point and Michigan was driving for the win. The Wolverines needed to convert a 3rd and 2nd to keep possession of the ball and keep the clock running.

Larry Station had something to say about that. He anticipated that the ball was going to Michigan's top running back, and he knew that the two linemen on the right side were All-Americans. He knew that the crucial down situation meant the best backs would run behind the best blockers. When the ball was snapped, Larry shut through the guard-tackle gap, meeting the Michigan running back 3 yards deep in the backfield. Got him. Michigan was forced to punt and Iowa took over for the final possession. The Hawkeyes drove down the field, managing the clock, and getting close enough for sophomore Rob Houghtlin to attempt a 29-yards field goal with just two seconds left on the clock. The kick was good, and Iowa won the game, 12–10. Anticipation.

The difference between failure and success is often the ability to anticipate the next play. Had Captain Smith and the White Star Line anticipated the potential danger present in the North Atlantic, adequate lifeboats would have been provided, lifeboat drills would have been run before heading out to sea, the lookouts would have had binoculars, and the iceberg warnings would have been taken seriously. These precautions may not have resulted in a safe voyage, but anticipating every possible reality would surely have prevented such a colossal loss.

The art of anticipation doesn't happen by accident. It is the result of responsible preparation and a commitment to doing what's right. When the world around us takes a turn and we find ourselves surrounded by icebergs, great peace of mind is found in knowing that we have prepared for the worst.

Photo Credit: UIowa Photo Service

Iowa linebacker Larry Station

When financial news of the 2008 economic crisis hit the airwaves, our country began scrambling for lifeboats. It was tempting for those of us at Berthel Fisher to do the same. Thankfully, we were able to remain cautiously optimistic because we make it a priority to know the positive, negative, and neutral factors in the industry, and we deal with that information honestly and ethically. When business is at its best, we guard against overconfidence by respecting potential pitfalls, and we never abandon sound fundamentals in search of shortcuts.

In an effort to calm the troops, I wrote a letter to our network of independent brokers, reminding them to stay focused and not to panic. "Keep doing what you do best," I wrote. "Uncertainties are creating many anxieties in the marketplace, so we will all need to keep alert. The greatest companies take advantage of these movements by sensing the opportunity and running with it."

The following day I received a reply from Jim, one of our registered representatives in North Carolina. He wrote:

> *Tom:*
> *Half a country away from you, here in central North Carolina, my pledge to you and BFCFS in general, is to maintain the integrity of my clients' investment base in our current, anxiety-provoking moment, and to continue to lay the foundation for successful wealth accumulation going forward.*

This message, along with many others, confirmed to me that our commitment to preparedness was getting through. Jim wasn't panicking or seeing the current crisis as an excuse to cut corners or find loopholes. Rather, he was focused on the best interests of his clients, in spite of market uncertainty.

Success lies in using what we know to anticipate what we don't know. Icebergs are considered hidden dangers because only about one-fifth of their mass can be seen above water, leaving most of the ice hidden beneath the surface.[11] Still, ship captains know that what they cannot see can still be deadly. The profound lessons of an unsinkable ship warn us all, on or off the sea, of the threat of unseen obstacles. Danger will always exist. The unexpected can always be expected. Deception and denial are not the answer to our problems. While they may offer temporary comfort, it is only through comprehensive and honest assessment that we are able to fully embrace the art of anticipation.

POSTGAME WITH COACH FRY

The art of anticipation

My experience in the Marine Corps exposed me to unprecedented discipline and a strong work ethic. Those drill instructors could have even taught my dad a thing or two. They taught us to be organized and prepared for anything. We learned that if we worked hard enough and prepared systematically, then we would be able to anticipate threats and increase the possibility of safety and success. We would be able to make the necessary adjustments, before danger arrived. In the Marine Corps, being properly prepared is truly a matter of life or death. It gave me a new appreciation for the concept of winning.

It saddens me to see so many young people today doing things sort of loosey-goosey. There's a general lack of discipline in our country these days, and it is very important that our young people learn the benefit of doing things a specific way. The military teaches great attention to detail and how to do things right the first time. Shortcuts are only for the ride to Grandma's house.

I loved everything about being a marine. It consistently gave me the feeling of being on the winning side, and I liked it. I will always have a great sense of pride about serving my country, and for all the men and women serving in our armed forces.

Football is obviously not a matter of life or death, but during my coaching years I consistently used the skills and leadership training I had received in the military. I learned never to take anything for granted, and I transferred that thinking to my players—or at least, I tried to. That 1979 Indiana game was a heartbreaker. I know we could've won it, if we would have just stayed focused on the game plan, but the boys hadn't yet learned how to handle winning. An individual or team must learn *how* to win.

I remember standing outside the locker room at halftime with my assistant coaches, hearing the players whoopin' and hollerin' and celebrating. "Gentlemen," I announced, "we've had a great first half, but I'm gonna tell you something: We're in real trouble. We have another half to play, and those boys in there can't take it mentally that we haven't won the game yet." I did my best to calm the team down, reminding them of Yogi Berra's words: "It ain't over till it's over." But it was too late. We lost the game and learned a great lesson.

Tom's right. When you don't take an honest look at short-comings and potential pitfalls, you leave room for stupid mistakes and all sorts of harmful thinking. I saw it happen over and over again all around me, and I was determined to keep it out of my coaching philosophy. Even though we had a few setbacks, I never stopped training my players and coaches to anticipate and prepare relentlessly.

My coaching staff at Iowa did a really good job of this. They trained our players to anticipate their opponents' next play, and Larry Station was one of our best. It's like he had a natural instinct to predict the next play.

During those last minutes of the 1985 Michigan game, Larry was able to make the big play because he'd done his homework. We hadn't called a blitz, so when Larry blitzed and crushed the ball carrier, I was pleasantly puzzled. I grabbed my headset and called Bill Brashier, my defensive coordinator, in the press box. "Coach," I barked, "did you have a blitz on?"

"No, Coach," Bill replied, sounding a little puzzled himself. "Larry did that all by himself." Obviously, our linebacker coach Barry Alvarez had done an outstanding job of coaching Larry Station in the art of anticipation.

It is absolutely impossible to be overprepared or to learn too much about the game you're playing. The unexpected should always be expected. Listen to me: All it takes is one lapse in focus for the tide to turn and the underdog to win. It's a little thing athletes like to call "an upset," and ship captains call "a tragedy."

9

DIVERSIFICATION

Achieving stability

HAYDEN PRIDED HIMSELF in creating an unpredictable football program on and off the field. Whether calling for a Bumerooski (fake punt) on fourth down, surprising opponents with the shotgun formation, or painting the visitors' locker room pink, Hayden was a master at diversifying his portfolio to gain a psychological edge. It was an edge that kept players interested, fans energized, and his opponents off balance.

Even though he didn't use a lot of trick plays during big games, everybody knew he had plenty of them stuffed up his sleeve, and it kept them guessing. Hayden created success at Iowa by building a football program that was as different as possible from the teams he coached against, while still staying fundamentally sound. This strategy required his opponents to completely change their practice routines just days prior to playing the

Hawkeye fake field goal

Hawkeyes. The Big Ten was known for playing aggressive, helmet-to-helmet football with tough physical defense. Smashmouth football. Hayden came along and spread his offensive formations across the field and had his tight ends stand in an upright stance in order to read the secondary coverage and relay it to the quarterback. He employed variety to create a winning program, and established a legacy at Iowa that still keeps opponents guessing today.

Each year, every college football team in every conference wants to win a national championship, but every season only one team claims the prize. In their pursuit, no coach relies solely on one player or one play to achieve success. They develop extensive playbooks with proven plays that stand the test of time, while

Photo Credit: UIowa Photo Service

incorporating new plays that shake things up a bit. They recruit and train a diverse group of offensive players, defensive players, and special teamers to get the job done. While certain players and plays are more central to success, they are only as good as the network that supports them.

Diversification in a football program doesn't guarantee a championship, but it does create stability and build endurance. It affords coaches and players the flexibility to adjust their strategy when faced with the unexpected. This creates a defensive posture that minimizes risk while protecting the goal/endzone. Just as diversification creates winning programs on the football field, it does the same thing in the boardroom. When markets are down, mistakes are made, or companies are faced with the unexpected, diversification is the insurance policy that keeps the ship afloat.

When I first started Berthel Fisher, I was often asked, "Why aren't you doing what other investment groups are doing?" Well, if I'd wanted to do what other investment groups were doing, I would have had no reason or desire to start my own. My goal has always been to minimize the investment risk of our customers by offering a diverse line of basic and alternative investment products. Diversification, not duplication.

In the early 1990s, Berthel Fisher began investing heavily in real estate. With our nation on a financial roller coaster and the bursting of the real estate bubble after the 1987 stock market crash, people thought we were crazy. In addition to Michael Jackson's "Thriller" and the craze of Cabbage Patch Kids, the eighties brought us double-digit inflation and the bombshell of Black Monday, when stocks dropped nearly 23 percent in a single day.[1] The early eighties saw interest rates soar to more than 18 percent,[2] largely due to the debt crisis of American farmers, and by the end of the decade, hundreds of savings and loans were failing, costing U.S. taxpayers more than $124 billion.[3] Sound familiar?

The savings and loan crisis was largely facilitated by the Tax Reform Act of 1986, which virtually eliminated federal tax incentives for real estate investors. It significantly reduced real estate values and ended the real estate boom of the eighties once and for all. The RTC was formed and the government again stepped in quietly to avert crisis.

Nevertheless, while most ran away from real estate, we ran to it. It wasn't a spontaneous decision. We spent a great deal of time and energy seeking expert advice, conducting personal research, and weighing the pros and cons. Once all of the facts had been considered, it was time to do a gut check. Regardless of data projections and popular opinion, was real estate the right decision? At the end of the day, our answer was yes.

Turns out, it was the ideal time to get in. The real estate we purchased in and since the early nineties has played a large roll in the stability of our company. Despite new financial crises and the latest wave of bank failures, we have landed on our feet, primarily due to diversification. However, the decrease in values of commercial real estate is taking its toll on investors and the real estate they purchased—not because they didn't diversify, but because we're in the worst debt crisis since the Great Depression.

All bets are off regarding the total economic fallout at this point. Our government's failure to regulate U.S. banks and Wall Street businesses will have negative ramifications for years to come, and the survival of some of our financial delivery systems is in doubt as new regulations sweep the nation.

It is vital that we learn from our mistakes, and some of the changes are definitely good. However, some will thwart the ingenuity of entrepreneurs, and it could take years for the dust to settle and the correction of excessive regulations to take place. Enforcing previous regulations would certainly have prevented greed from taking over, but they weren't enforced. As a result, the self-indulgence of a few reflects on the majority, and all of us will likely suffer the consequences of those managers who put "doing the right thing" on the shelf.

Companies that were solid before the crisis will default on loans and go broke, while those who survive will become even stronger and more elite. Stimulus measures will lead to more-conservative playbooks with less trick plays. After all, trick plays should only be used when they are based on solid research and ethics, and should never be used as shortcuts.

Greed and corruption, such as what we've seen in the Madoff scandal, serve to change the way even good businesses have to play the game. The problem is that those who were trusted took advantage of those who trusted them, and we have the problem our mothers warned us about. One bad apple has nearly spoiled the whole bunch. So, as Hayden did in the midst of tough football games, it's time to regroup and pull the team together.

While others flounder, we have to stick to our game plan. There is a key lesson here: Real estate was the right decision for us in the early nineties, but that doesn't mean it should consume our product portfolio today. Instead, it is a supplement to it. If we had made real estate our only investment, rather than meshing it into a diverse product collection, we would be taking a bath in it today. The 2008 Wall Street and credit crash has continued to cause significant problems in the overall real estate markets. Many products are doing okay, but others have had some issues as a result of the downturn.

Hayden calls this phenomenon "scratching where it itches." Having a diversified lineup, whether on the football field or in the boardroom, protects from downsides by allowing for flexibility, while also allowing for a big play or good investment return. When your top running back injures his knee, you'd better be able to "scratch where it itches" and deliver a new plan that keeps the team competitive. When real estate ends up in the tank, you'd better be able to "scratch where it itches" and rely on other investments to keep you afloat by getting the returns you need. The process of diversification doesn't always make sense to the crowd. It's not sexy because the goal isn't to get rich quick, but to build long-term stability. Nobody is right all of the time, and when things don't go as planned, you don't want to be forced to make an irrational decision. You want to have options.

In the investment arena, investment banking firms continually work to scratch where it itches in the quest for a winner. Sometimes it's successful and sometimes it fails. So, what really is the next big thing? Talk-show hosts; investment advisors; television news programs, newspapers, and magazines—they all make millions every year telling us what to buy, what to sell, and when.

It seems that the pursuit of gold at the end of the rainbow makes many of us content to run with the advice of the "experts" and forget to weigh their advice against our own scouting report. If you can't afford their advice, don't take it, regardless of how good it sounds. Hayden knew when and if he could take a risk on the field, and we must do the same so that we can all live to play another day.

This type of flexibility also provides the freedom to say "no" when something doesn't fit. Hayden turned down three coaching opportunities in the NFL because they weren't a good fit for him. He didn't want the hassle of a twenty-plus game schedule, and he wasn't interested in dealing with players who had sudden multimillionaire status. He didn't want to give up the joy of coaching college players and seeing them graduate. Because of the stability he created within his football program, he was never forced to make an irrational decision.

Every time I've allowed myself to get talked out of my defensive posture, to take a step away from the stability of diversification, I've ended up worse off. Several years ago, we owned a $200 million leasing company that was running exactly as planned. It was making money for us and our customers, and our brokers loved the business. Then, Wall Street showed up to show us a better way.

Over time, a few of our guys wanted more. They "knew the business" and convinced me to follow the advice of some Wall Street firms. They convinced me that we were missing a great opportunity to make more money in a shorter amount of time. Gut instinct told me to stick to the original game plan, protect our downside, and maintain a defensive posture, but I deferred to the experts who knew a lot about the leasing business, so I gave them the go-ahead to run with their ideas.

Three years later I woke up to multimillion-dollar losses and a huge headache. Our defensive posture was completely broken down and my original game plan was unrecognizable. Of course, the downturn in the telecommunications industry contributed to the damage. Because I had allowed myself to be romanced into chasing the fluff everyone said I was missing, instead of protecting our downside, I was forced to make the drastic decision to downsize the program at a huge loss. It still boggles my mind that I let myself get into that position, but I refuse to go through life mad about it. It taught me a valuable lesson about boundaries and balance, and in the long run, it made me a better leader.

Creating balance doesn't happen accidentally; it's a twofold process. First, it requires a deep commitment to a clear game plan. Second, it requires knowing when enough is enough. We have all seen winning college football programs get turned upside down in pursuit of a perfect season, and we have certainly seen profitable companies go down the tubes because people got greedy. Aren't there times when a 9–3 season is okay? Isn't it better to make a marginal yet dependable profit than to lose everything trying to make millions? Success absolutely requires risk, but it also requires knowing when enough is enough.

Hayden took plenty of risks throughout his coaching career, and he demanded excellence from himself, his coaches, and his players. He was never satisfied with mediocrity, but he refused to throw the baby out with the bathwater. When losses and missteps came, he didn't panic. He didn't throw out the game plan. He simply assessed the situation and made adjustments. He built enough diversity into the program to withstand a few bumps in the road, and he was never backed into a corner or forced to make an irrational decision. As a result, he left a solid legacy of success.

Hayden's record during his first season with the Hawkeyes was 5–6. The next year he finished 4–7. It wasn't until his third season at Iowa that Hayden and his Hawkeyes achieved a winning record of 8–4, earning the title of Big Ten Champions. It was Iowa's first winning season in more than twenty years.

Hayden coached two decades of Hawkeye football, finishing with a record of 143–89–6 and three Big Ten Championships. He led the Hawkeyes to fourteen bowl games, including three Rose Bowls, and became a member of the College Football Hall of Fame in 2003. Mostly, Hayden restored a winning tradition at Iowa that is still inspiring belief in Hawkeye fans, coaches, and

Coach Fry's Hall of Fame Certificate

players today. His strategy of diversifying on and off the football field led to a winning legacy and crowned him an Iowa icon.

With all of his accomplishments, Hayden never coached an undefeated season at Iowa, and I guarantee you that this fact is nowhere on his radar. He had a blast. His teams had a blast. They worked hard together, played hard together, and built a winning legacy together. It would have been a tragedy for Hawkeye players and fans to miss the glory days in search of greater "fluff."

If Hayden had been romanced by the money and stardom of the NFL, the story may have ended quite differently. If Iowa's Athletic Department had decided to dismiss Hayden in pursuit of the perfect season, an entire legacy of winning and a second generation of coaches may have been lost. Sometimes it's enough just to keep moving in the right direction.

You want to build a national championship team? Great. Tell me how you are going to do it. What is your offensive posture? What is your defensive posture? What are you going to do to make yourselves different from every other team in the league? How are you going to respond if it doesn't happen this season? Goals are not to be confused with strategy, and strategy must be multidimensional.

Several years ago, I began a system for tracking strategy that keeps me focused on action points vital to the goals I've set for my business and my personal life. Every year, I come up with a "Top Ten" list and write it on a piece of notebook paper that I keep folded in my pocket until all the items are checked off. Diversification is powerful, but it can also lead to an unhealthy split in focus. This system of visually tracking short-term

Tom with Hawkeye Mascot, Herky

objectives keeps me moving in the right direction and maintains my psychological edge. Writing it down also makes it a commitment. I may not have a pink locker room, but Hayden inspires me to do what's necessary to sustain a diverse playbook that creates stability, keeps our customers energized, and always strives for a winning record. Trust me, disappointment will come, but knowing your game plan will keep you focused and motivated. What is your game plan?

POSTGAME WITH COACH FRY

Diversification

My first game at Iowa was against Indiana. When the guys lined up for the first snap of the ball, we didn't put anybody in the backfield but the quarterback and one running back, with the rest of the guys spread across the field. The stadium went nuts.

For years, Hawkeye fans watched their offense clump together in a Wing-T formation, and for years it was unsuccessful. When the fans caught a glimpse that we were changing things up a bit and adding some variety to our playbook, they were excited. Even our athletic director, Bump Elliot, hollered "Holy cow!" from the press box when he heard the crowd's thunderous approval. Diversification creates enthusiasm, keeps your opponents guessing, and leads to greater success.

Photo Credit: Ted Roeder

Iowa fans celebrate a touchdown

Of course, mixing things up didn't lead to instant perfection for the Hawkeyes. We were trying to rebuild the program and establish greater stability, and it was working. However, there were fans and reporters looking for any reason to doubt. Shirley and I even had some fans come by our home on the Coralville Reservoir. They were in their boat, yelling through a megaphone, and calling me all sorts of names—even threatening me—after a game that we had actually won. What is wrong with people? Apparently, we hadn't beat the point spread.

Fortunately, most Iowa fans have shown great appreciation for what we were trying to do, and it was a great thrill to watch their reactions. There will always be a few pessimists in the crowd, and it's a mistake if you let them get you down. The view is pretty good from the cheap seats, and Monday-morning quarterbacking has become a sport in itself, whether in sports, politics, or business. As a leader, you have to be confident in the changes you make, teach your team to ignore the bull from the cynics, and stay the course. Do that, and winning will take care of itself.

Changing things up, creating diversity in your game plan, requires a great deal of discipline and patience: discipline to avoid haphazard decisions and patience to give your plan time to work. Success doesn't usually come overnight, but if you stick with a plan, the rewards will come. One of my most gratifying moments in coaching was watching Hawkeye fans celebrate their first Big Ten Championship.

In my personal life and in coaching, I'm not crazy about playing it safe. Don't get me wrong: Although I don't believe in taking unnecessary risks, it's not productive to play it safe all the time. There has to be some variety in order to create enthusiasm and to keep your players from getting bored. We had a lot of fun keeping the players and fans on their toes and keeping the opposition wondering what on earth we might do next. Maintaining a diverse program produced both the stability and the excitement we needed in order to create a winning program.

Incidentally, I took the same approach in my personal business. Shirley and I have achieved a certain amount of financial stability by diversifying our portfolio and staying away from get-rich-quick temptations. It's been a lot of fun fiddling with the stock market over the years, buying nickel-and-dime stocks, because I've established limits for myself and never pay more than four bucks a share.

A segment of the market that really interests me, probably because of my personal fight with cancer, is the biochemical and medical segment. When someone is finally able to say, "Hey, this is going to cure cancer," their stock will go through the roof. So, I like to pick three of these stocks each year that are no more than four bucks apiece. Sometimes I choose a new company; sometimes it's an up-and-coming company; but whatever I buy, it's the result of hours of research. I always do my homework before investing and I never like to follow the crowd.

I once paid $3.25 for a stock, just prior to a bout with cancer. With two cancer operations in the five months that followed, I wasn't able to pay much attention to the market. Later, I discovered that $3.25 had turned into $70 a share. Sad to say, I didn't catch it until it was back down to $27, and it was down to $24 by the time I got it sold. Still, it was a nice "little" six-figure profit. Wish they'd all turn out that way.

At the moment, I'm working on a nice little land deal (or at least I hope it's nice). With the recent real estate dip, I was able to purchase a property for $120,000 that had been worth $425,000 just a few years ago. When things start coming back to normal with the economy, it should lead to a considerable profit.

Whether on the football field or in the boardroom, a leader has to look at all the options, even the ones that seem absurd at first. You just never know what strategy is going to be the most effective, but one thing's for certain: If you keep doing the same unsuccessful things over and over, you will continue to be unsuccessful. Don't be afraid to take a risk—to mix things up a bit. Finding "luck" and making successful decisions comes from diligent research, educating yourself thoroughly, and being willing to think outside the box. You see, I'm not all that smart, but I pay attention.

10

UNCOMPROMISING CHARACTER

Defining the nonnegotiables

OUR GOVERNMENT HAS been strapped with the economic challenge of paying for the missteps of a large portion of the financial services industry. Millions of Americans watched as the news of the economic "bailout" quickly turned to the more politically correct "rescue package." We watched as AIG thanked us by using a portion of their $85 billion emergency loan to pay for a lavish retreat for top producers. Nearly half a million dollars was spent on the trip, including $16,000 for just one presidential suite, $23,380 for spa treatments, $6,939 for golf, and $9,980 for room service and cocktails.[1] In the weeks that followed, more excesses were reported, but each one was quickly excused by the chairman and CEO of AIG. As I watched the news coverage, I questioned whether or not this was necessary. If the trip was required or simply could not be canceled, then why the excesses?

Beyond Xs and Os

According to a 2005 article in *The Wall Street Journal*, serious questions were being raised about the integrity of AIG's financial reporting systems, including checks and balances in their accounting process, years before taxpayers were called upon to supply emergency funds.[2] In the wake of their questionable business practices and no appearance of remorse, our government agreed to increase the loan to AIG, nearly doubling the original $85 billion handout. Since then, more problems have been popping up. I do not question the importance of entertaining and rewarding top performers, but I do question why adjustments are not made when someone else's money is being spent.

Here is my concern about accepting ownership of one's decisions: I love my children very much, and, like all parents, Deanna and I are incredibly proud when we see them working hard and displaying integrity. If they ever need help, we will be there for them. Simply for the sake of illustration, let's pretend for a moment that our children find themselves financially destitute after making several compromising decisions that are contrary to the sound business principles they have learned. Knowing they messed up, I affirm my confidence in them by providing the necessary funds to get them back on track.

A few days after issuing the "emergency loan," I stop by their apartment, expecting to find them hard at work, trying to earn some money and to regain my trust. Instead, I find them playing with a brand-new, state-of-the-art video-game system, on a brand-new big-screen plasma television, and reclining on a brand-new leather couch. Hmmm. Let's just say, that's where ownership comes in. Everyone makes decisions that cause losses

President's Club Conference

now and then. It's a fact of life. The question you have to ask yourself is: Will you cut your losses and take ownership of the problem by adjusting spending patterns, or will you wait for someone else to rescue you and then mismanage the funds for your own comfort?

There is nothing fundamentally wrong with most purchases. It is the timing of expenditures and the overall management of funds that is called into question. When you are charged with the responsibility of managing funds and talent, then you must learn from each mistake and make better decisions the next time. It will serve you well as you go through life. Once you have succeeded and commitments have been honored, then you can reward yourself—because then, you will deserve it.

Our company prides itself on rewarding top producers with luxurious incentives. Our men and women work their tails off every year to achieve personal success and to assist their customers in achieving and preserving personal wealth. As a result, our company remains profitable and we continue to grow. This sort of individual achievement warrants reward and recognition. There is nothing wrong with incentives. In fact, they are the hallmark of the sales industry.

AIG, which received emergency funds from the government, is also accustomed to rewarding top producers. In fact, their financial planners generated almost $200 million in revenue during the first half of 2008, and they certainly deserved recognition.[3] When I watched and read the reports of this company's extravagant expenditures, after receiving the first $85 billion from taxpayers, I couldn't help but ask myself how our company would have handled the situation. It's easy to point fingers, to look at the faults of others through a magnifying glass while failing to notice our own, so I used this headline story as an opportunity to do some soul-searching. As Hayden would say, I used it as a tool to scout my team, and I encourage you to do the same.

Before drawing any conclusions, we have to define the non negotiables and determine what integrity really looks like. What is it that companies and individuals must have—or do, or be—in order to pass the character test?

During my junior year at St. Ambrose College, I decided to pursue a part-time job at Hawkeye Honda, selling motorcycles and four-wheelers. Because my mom and dad were raising thirteen kids and weren't able to help much with college, I needed some extra cash to cover my living expenses. I went to get a haircut and then headed to the dealership. Within minutes of being introduced to Mr. Bickford, the store manager, I was fully aware that he didn't like my shaggy 1970s hairstyle, even after the haircut. He was a military man, his head practically shaved, and I rarely saw him crack a smile. Even so, he told me to come back in a couple of weeks.

Two weeks later, I was back in Mr. Bickford's office. He still wasn't sure. They needed salespeople but it wasn't really a job for a college student. It would only pay minimum wage (about $2 an hour) and just 2 percent commission. As I listened to Mr. Bickford try to convince me that I didn't want to work there, I interrupted him and said plainly, "Okay, here's the deal. I'll get my hair cut and I'll work for you for two weeks. If you don't like me at the end of the two weeks, you don't have to pay me a dime." It was no longer a risk for Mr. Bickford. Two years later I was still there, making more than some of the full-time sales guys.

Before leaving the dealership, Mr. Bickford asked if I was interested in taking *his* job. I loved the people and the freedom, but it was time for me to move on and pursue my own "coaching" job.

I took a risk when I walked into Hawkeye Honda that first day, banking on my work ethic to carry me, and it worked. (I imagine the walk-ons at Iowa during Hayden's tenure felt much the same way.) The power and effectiveness of hard work and fearless dedication should never be underestimated.

One day I noticed a customer who was being ignored. He was a scruffy-looking guy who worked at the John Deere factory, and he came in periodically to look at the same big English bike. It had a price tag of a little more than $2,000, which was a lot of money for a bike in those days. After one particularly long look at the bike, he stuffed his hands in his pockets, quietly left the bike in the showroom, and headed out the door. Something just didn't seem right, so I followed him out.

By the time I reached him, he was already in the driver's seat of his car, so I knocked on the window. "Sir," I said, "is everything all right? You've been looking at that bike for a long time." He rolled down his window, revealing a check from his credit union. He started to explain how long he had been saving and how much he had saved each week. "Well, I want to buy that bike in there, but I know your boss won't budge on the price, and I'm a few bucks short." Sure enough, the customer everyone ignored because they thought he was broke was holding a check that was almost enough to pay for the bike, taxes, and licensing—almost. I chuckled and invited him to come back inside, assuring him that we'd work something out.

The other salespeople were amazed. The biggest sale of the month came from the most unlikely customer, to the part-time college guy. It's the lesson Hayden teaches others: Never underestimate anyone. Sometimes the walk-on player is the one who ends up in the NFL.

Digging graves, mowing lawns, delivering mail with my grandfather, and sweeping floors were significant training grounds for my experience at the Honda dealership. I was not willing to accept "no" for an answer, and I was determined to do whatever it took to prove myself. It is this strong sense of personal determination that motivated me to risk working for free for two weeks. It is what motivated me to follow the factory worker to his car, even though it seemed so futile to others. Talent and education are important, but they cannot replace good, old-fashioned work ethic or personal instinct.

The first nonnegotiable, then, is hard work. During football season, Hayden is all football. He coached before the time-saving tools of digital film, computer spreadsheets, electronic playbooks, and scouting software were available. Still, he did what it took to get the job done, spending long hours for months on end to be sure his team was prepared. Hayden expected his players and coaches to give 110 percent at all times, and he expected even more than that from himself.

Licensed psychologist Dr. Paul White identifies seven characteristics of a good work ethic: dependability, punctuality, following instructions, staying on task (even when no one is watching), doing quality work (going above and beyond), having a positive "can-do" attitude, and solving problems creatively with a determination to overcome obstacles.[4]

Many in the workforce today have developed an entitlement mentality. They have fancy degrees from prestigious schools. They graduated with honors. They are the son or daughter of so-and-so. They are entitled to be wined and dined, to have an impressive title with a six-figure income. Accommodating this "you owe me" mentality, instead of cultivating an attitude of ownership and a willingness to work from the bottom up, has led to some bloated salaries, top-heavy corporations, and lavish benefit programs. It has led to greed.

Greed is a funny thing. To some degree, we all experience it. If kept in check, it can motivate. If not, it will destroy, and the current housing and debt crisis is a perfect example. History will show that many people in government, the banking industry, and on Wall Street allowed greed to infringe on good judgment. Everyone wanted housing sales to continue and it made the economy look good. In the process of fighting a war, we were fueling a financial meltdown. Bigger homes, second homes, investment properties. Money was easier than ever to get, and greed took over. We exchanged good old-fashioned work ethic for get-rich-quick schemes.

We cannot negotiate our principles. People and companies of character do the right thing, every time, without question.

We have a character crisis in our country today. Five minutes on Google reveals football players in Florida suspended for an on-campus fight, an athlete in West Virginia arrested for a stabbing, a college president in Michigan arrested for driving under the influence, a high school teacher in Texas arrested on drug charges, an executive in New York charged with embezzlement, and a sheriff indicted on federal conspiracy charges.[5] The list goes on and on and on. No city, state, or occupation is exempt.

Doing what's right is rarely the easiest or most profitable course of action. It often costs more, takes longer, and sacrifices the adrenaline rush. But, it almost always results in long-term gain. I've never heard of anyone apologizing for sticking to an ethical standard of behavior.

The owner of Hawkeye Honda, Wayne, was developing a beautiful piece of property just off Interstate 80, near the banks of the Mississippi. One afternoon Wayne says to me, "Hey, Tom,

Tom with his wife, Deanna, in 2008

how are things going with Deanna?" Now remember, I was a college student, so I just sort of kicked at the floor and said, "Uh, I don't know. I think I'm prob'ly gonna marry her."

Next thing I know, Wayne takes out his property development sheet and starts pointing at it. "You and Deanna need this lot right here by the lake when you get married." Wow. He had plans for me.

Even though I was doing okay selling motorcycles on the side, I certainly didn't have $8,000 to buy an empty lot. "Well," I sort of laughed, "sounds good to me, Wayne, but all I have to borrow against is my little Volkswagen in the parking lot, and my drum set."

He explained that I would only need to put $1,000 down, and only after I graduated from St. Ambrose the following spring. It would be at least another year, maybe two, before the land would be ready to go, and the balance wouldn't be due until then. "Sounds like a great deal," I said. "Where do I sign?"

Tom Berthel with his drum set

Wayne had me initial the lot on the map and then looked at me. "Tom," he said, "your initials are on the lot. It's yours."

Several months later, just before graduation, Wayne came back to me and announced that he had some great news about his land. The entire plot next to it had been purchased by John Deere for a new plant. "It's worth a lot of money," he said. Then he asked if I'd sell it for the $16,000 a new buyer was offering.

What? I'd never given him a dime. I'd never signed a thing. But a few weeks later I had a check in my hand for $16,000, minus the $8,000 I never gave him. That's integrity. He stuck to his word even when it would have been easy not to.

All of a sudden, Deanna and I (we were engaged by then) had enough money to put down on a house, with enough left over to get me started in business. The economy was terrible and interest rates were sky high, but because Wayne was a man of his word we were off to a great start.

When you are a person or company of character, you do what you say you're going to do. You do not look for a way to cut corners or exploit a good deal at the expense of others. There may be times when certain things are beyond your control, and you may still get blamed for whatever goes wrong. However, don't deliberately sacrifice long-term success and a trustworthy reputation for short-term gain and a cloud of suspicion. You play the game with integrity, period.

When the U.S. Treasury agreed to hand out even more of your money and mine to a company that didn't appear to be showing much restraint or gratitude, it came with a stern

Tom and Deanna Berthel early in his career

167

warning from assistant secretary Neel Kashkari, who instructed the company to "comply with stringent limitations on executive compensation for its top executives, golden parachutes, its bonus pool, corporate expenses and lobbying."[6]

I agree with Mr. Kashkari, but after scouting my own team and identifying the nonnegotiables of integrity, I have a question: Why in the world do we have to warn against these excesses? And what is happening to our moral conscience—to the internal barometer that appeals to our sense of decency? Many financial service companies have negotiated integrity for the sake of profit, and it has caused a colossal breakdown in consumer trust.

The conclusion of our scouting report, then, is that a good work ethic causes us to roll up our sleeves and work harder in the face of adversity. Our commitment to doing what is right causes us to make decisions with the interests of every client and every employee in mind, not just those of the executive team.

Uncompromising character is a rare attribute these days. It is an attribute that our grandparents demanded and our parents expected. Let it also be an attribute that we restore for the sake of our children and grandchildren. If we don't do it, who will?

POSTGAME WITH COACH FRY

Uncompromising character

I grew up with a clear set of rules. One thing my father did very clearly was to define the nonnegotiables in our family, and we cooperated for our own well-being. Sadly, I've seen lots of changes over the years. It seems so prevalent now that people have their hands out all the time instead of having the personal conviction and work ethic to earn their own way. When we no longer have to perform in order to be rewarded, a sort of laziness sets in and competition is devalued.

This attitude of entitlement was not allowed on my teams under any circumstances. I found that it was good for the guys to realize that they had to earn everything they got. Nobody was going to hand it to them, and this made them especially proud of their accomplishments. Today, guys like that stand out. There are so many loafers that the competition isn't really that great anymore. Character really stands out.

I am so troubled when I hear about all the bad things going on with players today. When we were recruiting, we determined and communicated our expectations right upfront. On the first day of practice I told my guys, "Gentlemen, these are the things you have to do in order to win, and these are the things you have to do in order to lose." I'd list everything very clearly: 1, 2, 3, and so on. Then I'd point to the losing list and say, "You can do these things over here if you want to, but you just can't be on my football team."

My rules were clear and nonnegotiable, and they included actions on and off the football field. They were not allowed to wear earrings or let their shirttails hang out of their pants. There was a whole list of things like this that are, in my opinion, very commonsense and responsible things for them to live up to. Most guys took great pride in knowing what they *could* do and what they *couldn't* do. We were developing character and confidence.

As a deep-divin' Baptist—which means I got baptized in the bottom of a Texas creek and came up with mud in my ears—my folks never allowed me to make excuses for bad decisions. Whether you come from high society or the wrong side of the tracks, you have to live a certain way and do certain things in order to build lasting success.

Young people need to have role models with good character and integrity. This is how they catch the vision to become winners in every sense of the word, not just on the scoreboard or in their bank accounts, but deep within themselves. Growing up, I was very blessed to have coaches and teachers who were excellent role models for me. And then in my coaching years, I had players and assistant coaches who inspired me with their convictions and integrity.

As an American, U.S. Marine, and world history teacher, I find that the ideals of our nation's founders have been very influential in developing my convictions. Quite frankly, I can't understand for the life of me why there has been such a shift in our thinking from those days to now. My generation learned quickly that hard work and integrity are rewarded, while laziness and dishonesty are not.

I often wonder what America is coming to. Even if hand-outs are well-intentioned, where do they stop? How does a government determine who is worthy of help and who isn't? It interferes with the natural order of things. The problem with a government that wants everything to be fair is that sooner or later you run out of other people's money to spend.

If one of my guys wasn't giving his best effort on the football field, or he made a stupid decision downtown, then he didn't get the reward of playing on Saturday. Simple as that, and it was no surprise to him. Expectations were clear and consistent. My guys found great comfort in understanding exactly what to do and what not to do, and they found great pride in living by the rules of the team. It's how we're wired. I never had a problem with laziness or indifference on my teams because I never rewarded it. I don't care if you're the greatest quarterback on earth; if you don't give me everything you've got and you compromise your principles, then you don't get to play. On the contrary, if a player (or a company) gives 100 percent every day, sacrificing of themselves and looking out for the best interests of others, success will come. One way or another, success will come.

11

ADVERSITY AS OPPORTUNITY

Pressing on

ADVERSITY. MISFORTUNE. HARD times. It's the stuff every one of us must face, without exception, and no matter what life throws at us, we can take comfort in knowing that tough times don't last, and tough people can emerge from trials with greater strength and motivation for what lies ahead. At the heart of every obstacle lies an opportunity, waiting to be discovered.

In previous chapters we've discussed the importance of maintaining a positive, winning attitude in the midst of adversity and the benefit of being surrounded with head-coach types and optimists. There are many precautions that can be taken in order to minimize the damage of tough times, but when the going gets *really* tough—when the cancer treatments are tearing us up or the economy has stripped us of everything we've worked so hard for—it isn't enough to grit our teeth and endure the struggle with a forced smile. No; we must find the courage deep within ourselves to actually embrace pain as an avenue for growth and an opportunity to inspire others.

Everyone loves to hear a good ol' rags-to-riches story. It's greatly inspiring to hear how a poor farm boy from Texas, raised on the wrong side of the tracks, became a famous college football coach. It is captivating to see Olympic athletes beat overwhelming odds in order to compete and then stand on the podium draped in gold and covered in tears of victory. This tendency to be inspired by triumph over adversity is part of our human nature, and it's why television shows such as *Extreme Makeover: Home Edition* and *The Biggest Loser* are so wildly popular.

Even though we desire happy endings and want them to come quickly, it cannot be forgotten that the pain we endure in the midst of adversity may be the very thing—the essence of motivation—that shoves us toward our destiny.

In 1945, Hayden and twelve of his classmates embraced their underdog status in the one-class Texas high school football system, and grabbed adversity by the tail. It was their senior year at Odessa High School, in a small oil-well town populated by roughnecks and roustabouts, and their final football season had been a disappointment. Their goal was to win the state championship, but they ended up losing in the quarterfinals.

Not to be defeated, Hayden and his teammates decided to continue their pursuit of a winning season, despite one seemingly immovable obstacle: high school graduation. "We lived tough lives in that little town," Hayden recalls, "and that toughness spilled over into everything we did. We did whatever it took to be successful."

At that time in Texas, any high school student who hadn't graduated or turned nineteen by September would still be eligible to participate in athletics. Seeing this as a golden opportunity Hayden and a number of his teammates who still had to complete senior English, chose to take the course in the fall in order to give them one more shot. This last-chance season ended in fourteen consecutive wins, 400 points scored, and a mere 50 points allowed to the opposition. Not only did they have an undefeated season, but they also won the state championship in 1946.

Tom working on 1987 offerings

Even though Hayden admits that football is not a matter of life and death, giving up on your dreams can be. Sometimes we just have to look an obstacle square in the eye and go for it, even if it doesn't make sense to the rest of the world.

Golf is also not a matter of life and death. A good shot can make you feel alive and a bad shot at the worst moment can make you feel like you want to die, but at the end of the day, it's just a game.

Several years ago, I had the opportunity to combine my love for golf with my love for chasing dreams when a group of us decided to spotlight the beauty of Iowa by building Iowa's first public championship golf course. It was going to be fun. With the stock market stronger than ever, we decided to take the project public and began meeting with potential investors immediately. The minimum offering of $4 million would have to be raised in just a few months, so we had no time to waste. There was much enthusiasm for the project, and with just a couple of weeks to go we had raised nearly $3.5 million. This was a great accomplishment, but we still needed to scare up the remaining half-million.

It came to my attention that there was a doctor in Florida who was interested in our project, so I gave him a call on Friday, and by Sunday afternoon I was on a plane to Florida. His office was beautiful and his enthusiasm certain. We visited only an hour before he committed $500,000, enough to make the project a reality. Everything was going just perfectly. Too perfectly.

He left to retrieve his checkbook only to return a few moments later with a newspaper and a pale face. "Have you seen what happened to the markets today?" My mind started churning.

The markets dipped a bit on Friday, but nothing alarming. What in the world was going on? Before I could reply, he flashed me the headlines and said, "We've just had the largest one-day decline in stock market history, almost twenty-three percent. Five hundred billion dollars, gone. I just lost a lot of money, Tom."

I could hardly believe what I was hearing. *Was it true? And if it was, what did it mean for the golf course project? More important, what did it mean for my investment company?* In just minutes, extreme excitement about raising half a million dollars turned to extreme bewilderment as our new investor expressed second thoughts, and understandably so.

The two of us began processing the news and were soon back to discussing the golf course. "You know what?" he finally said. "You are a nice guy, and you seem to know what you're doing. I can't give you the whole $500,000, but I'll write you a check for $250,000 right now." Cool. I was honored to have his trust and thrilled to have the investment. Still, it left us more than a quarter of a million from our goal, with only four days left to raise it. I graciously accepted the check and headed back to Iowa.

As they say, close only counts in horseshoes and hand grenades. With the devastation of Black Monday, we were unable to close the deal which was set for that Thursday. We fell short of our goal, and scheduled a press conference to notify Iowans that we would return the nearly $3.75 million we had raised and put our dream of building the championship course on hold.

In hindsight, we should have bought the remaining units, as it would have worked great for the project. The course has had its share of struggles, but it is open and beautiful. None of us knows

Amana Colonies Golf Course

for sure how it will look in the end, but the legacy of building it lives on.

I was sick, but I knew we couldn't give up in the face of this adversity. It was a worthy goal for Iowa, and I was more committed than ever. We decided to pull together and back a loan for the $4 million needed to build the course, and there was a local banker who was willing to work with us. It was a huge risk considering just one of every ten venture-capital projects succeeds, but we were not willing to give up on the opportunity to bring such an exciting project to Iowa. Our hearts were in it, so we stared the obstacles square in the eye and went for it.

Since the Amana Colonies Golf Course opened for play in 1989, it has been rated consistently in top public golf courses

In the news

in Iowa and the nation, and has received a four-star rating by *Golf Digest*. Mostly, it is a dream fulfilled. Those involved with the course have been privileged to share in the dreams of many nonprofit organizations, helping to continue the vital services they provide. This year, Miracles in Motion will host its ninth annual golf tournament at the Amana Colonies course, raising funds to support an extensive program using horse-related activities to provide therapy, education, and recreation to hundreds of people with disabilities each year. Our partnership with this organization, and others like it, combined with the great people I have met and the wonderful sense of state pride the course provides, make me so thankful that we persevered through adversity and seized the opportunity, even though it may not have made sense to the rest of the world.

Since then I have been involved in hundreds of millions of dollars' worth of capital raises and investment sales. Our partici-pation in syndications with many companies in real estate, company equities, debt issues, and energy raises has been extraor-dinary. I never dreamed we would make the nationwide scene in the investment business. It makes me incredibly proud that our efforts have fueled economic growth. It isn't always the largest companies that make a difference.

Not long before we decided to develop the Amana course, Iowa farmers faced the greatest economic drought in the history of the Midwest. The eighties brought high interest rates and a drop in farmland value of nearly 60 percent. Farm families tried desperately to pay off debt before asset values plummeted, but, in most cases, were unable to do so. Record harvests created crop surpluses and drove prices down, which, for the first time in history, resulted in total interest payments on farm loans exceeding total net farm income. To make matters worse, President Carter's foreign grain embargo took a large chunk of the overseas market away from American farmers.[1]

The pain experienced by family farmers was immeasurable and the human cost high. Foreclosures, suicides, homicides, increased domestic violence, divorce, and substance abuse were all part of the fallout. Even though it was a national and historic crisis, many Americans were still unaware of its significance.

As American farms plunged, Hawkeye football was making a comeback. In 1981, Iowa overcame twenty non-winning seasons and restored a winning record, claiming their first conference championship since sharing the title with Minnesota in 1960. The eighties were great years for Iowa football. Hayden's Hawkeyes were ranked number one in the AP poll for the first time in twenty-four years, played in eight consecutive bowl games (the longest bowl-streak in Hawkeye history), and claimed three conference championships. In addition, Hayden had the privilege of coaching All-American quarterback Chuck

Photo Credit: Ulowa Photo Service

The 1981 Iowa Hawkeyes

Long and All-American linebacker Larry Station. A winning spirit had returned to Kinnick Stadium, but Hayden has never been one to bask in the glory. He is continually looking for ways to do more, both on and off the football field.

These years brought great media attention to Iowa football, along with a growing number of fans across the nation. With Iowa being a leading agricultural state, Hayden realized that he and his players had an obligation to use their success as a means to draw attention to the economic hardship of American farmers.

On October 19, 1985, at the height of the farm crisis and the Hawkeyes' success, number-one Iowa played number-two

Coach Fry with Larry Station and Chuck Long

Michigan at Kinnick Stadium. It was advertised as the game of the century, nationally televised by CBS and commentated by Brent Musburger and former Notre Dame head coach, Ara Parseghian. Hayden was thrilled to use the pregame attention to support and encourage American farmers by displaying ANF decals (America Needs Farmers) on each player's helmet. The decals were yellow, about half the size of the Tigerhawk logo, and placed high on the right side of the helmets to optimize exposure to the cameras.

Iowa beat Michigan that day, creating one of the greatest moments in Hawkeye history. More importantly, though, a great deal of publicity was directed to hardworking American farmers, and many news stories popped up in national newspapers and sports magazines.

Although the direct benefit of the ANF decal could never be quantified, sportswriter Andy Hamilton of *The Daily Iowan* recognized it this way: "For three hours every fall Saturday, Hayden Fry and his Iowa football team were a remedy for the blues. Fry understood what Iowans were going through and he showed how much he cared for their hard work."[2]

The ANF decals remained part of the Hawkeyes' uniforms until 1993, when the National Collegiate Athletic Association declared them in violation of NCAA football equipment rules and ordered them removed. All Hayden could say was a frustrated, "Isn't that unbelievable?"[3] Though the ANF decals cost the Hawkeyes very little in effort or expense, they celebrated the fighting spirit that inspires people to press on in the face of adversity, and they represent one of Hayden's proudest accomplishments.

It's easy to see problems as "too big." We think to ourselves, *What can I possibly do to make a difference?* Let's face it: The racial integration of college football in the 1960s and the farm crisis of the 1980s were way bigger than Hayden Fry. Stock market crashes and historic floods are way bigger than me or my company. It is very easy to sit back and wait for someone else to fix big problems, but it is important to remember that it isn't so much a solution people are looking for as it is the will to believe that things will get better and the comfort of knowing that somebody cares. Tough times are inevitable, but we must look them square in the eye with a fighting spirit. When everything around us seems bleak and we're tempted to throw our hands up in defeat, the

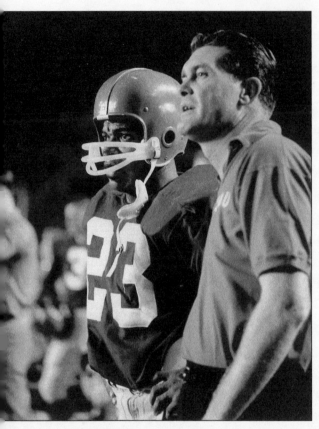

Coach Fry with Jerry LeVias

presence of a fighting spirit has immeasurable power to inspire hope.

During his tenure at SMU, Jerry LeVias was spit on, some teammates wouldn't share the same showers with him, and alumni withdrew their support from the university.[4] Jerry underwent surgery in 1967, after an opponent crushed three bones in his eye socket during a pileup. "My trademark was not to get tackled by more than one person so as not to end up under the pile," he told reporters. "I tried to survive because I knew the things that would happen if I stayed on the ground a long time."[5]

One year later, during the 1968 season, an opposing team's lineman spit in Jerry's face, spewing racial obscenities and screaming at him to "go home." It was the only time Jerry ever lost it on the football field. He stormed off, threw his helmet against the concrete wall, and told Hayden, "I quit. I'm not going to take this anymore." Who could blame him? Most of us would have gone home years earlier.

In all his coaching years, Hayden never tolerated quitting, and he knew this was a personal battle Jerry couldn't afford to lose. Regardless of the score at the end of the game, this was a fight against the injustice of every black athlete—past, present, and future—and they had come way too far to give up now. Without sentiment or flowery consolation, Hayden simply said, "Don't let your teammates down, son, and don't let that guy beat you."

Realizing that his team had just held TCU at the 38-yard line and was preparing to receive the punt, Jerry said, "Coach, I'm going to run this one back all the way," and ran onto the field. Being the sort of competitor Hayden is, Jerry's conviction must have sent chills down his spine.

One kick and 89 yards later, Jerry crossed the goal line to score the winning touchdown. This was just one of many outstanding football plays in Jerry's career. During his college days, he led SMU to their first conference football title in eighteen years, was named athletic and academic All-American in 1968, was a first team All Southwest Conference selection three times, and held most of the league's receiving records for nearly two decades (with 155 receptions for 2,275 yards and 22 touchdowns). Jerry went on to play six years in the NFL and still holds the SMU receiving records for most receptions in a game (15), receiving yards in a game (213), and receiving yards in a season (1,131).[6]

These are impressive statistics, worthy of the place they earned for him in the College Football Hall of Fame in 2003, but it is Jerry's fighting spirit that causes Hayden to say, "Jerry LeVias was a great player and a better person. He paved the way for a lot of players who followed, and so many of them still owe him a huge debt of gratitude."

Photo Credit: UIowa Photo Service

Iowa's 1982 Rose Bowl Team

There are surely times when Jerry must question whether the personal pain and adversity he endured during those years was worth it, but he persevered. He looked past the pain and found an opportunity to make a difference. His fighting spirit revolutionized college football and continues to inspire athletes today.

He's just one guy. If he hadn't fought through the adversity, maybe someone else would have, but think of what he would have missed. Because he found the courage deep within himself to embrace the struggle and seize the opportunity in adversity, he inspired the world.

Happy endings are never guaranteed, and overcoming adversity isn't always pretty. Jerry calls his record-breaking, 89-yard punt return in 1968 the "least satisfying of his career" because it wasn't the result of his love for the game but his anger toward an opponent. But, he didn't quit. He picked up his helmet and ran back onto the field. That is where our destinies are found—in the defining moments when we say to ourselves, "I'm running this one back all the way."

With Hayden's leadership, Iowa broke losing streaks against Purdue (20 games), Ohio State (16 games), and Michigan (9 games). He restored a winning tradition at Iowa that many thought was impossible, but success didn't keep cancer from invading Hayden's body. No success is a vaccine against adversity. As long as we are breathing, adversity will try to beat us, and for every success story there are a thousand defeats. If we want to make a difference in life and inspire others, then we must search tirelessly for opportunity when tough times come.

It wasn't until many years after he had coached Jerry LeVias that I met Hayden, and several more years after that before I would call him a friend. Even so, I can just imagine the subtle and satisfied smirk that must have appeared on Hayden's face every time Jerry put points on the board, scoring one more victory against violence and hatred. Hayden seized the opportunity to use his success as a football coach as a voice for his childhood buddies. It was his way of speaking on behalf of their pain and engaging a fighting spirit to make the world a better place.

POSTGAME WITH COACH FRY

Adversity as opportunity

Aw, Levi. That kid endured more adversity in one football season than most people endure in an entire lifetime, and he did it with exceptional dignity. I love him like a son.

The day Jerry and I sat together, in his parents' home, neither of us dreamed how bad it was really going to be. Of course we knew it would be difficult. That's why we screened players for two years before we found Jerry. We were searching for a student athlete who was determined and dedicated to achieving his goal of getting a degree. He had to have the skills to be a player. Sitting on the bench wouldn't do. Finally, he had to have real thick skin in order to deal with the tough stuff ahead.

When I was in his home for the first time, Jerry pulled out a New Testament and quoted a couple scriptures to me. I don't remember what scriptures they were, but it was fantastic, and I was so impressed by it. That was the moment I knew we were on to something. Years later, I asked Levi if he remembered doing that and he just said, "Coach Fry, all I remember is that my momma was cooking dinner for us. You smelled the food and went back to the kitchen. Once you got back there you started telling her how to cook those beans."

Levi and I didn't talk football much during the recruiting process. I knew he was a player and he was smart enough to know that he would be a groundbreaker for black athletes in the Southwest Conference. Instead, we talked about his goals in life, beyond college, and about the importance of getting his education. I was very truthful with him about the potential adversity, but I never dreamed that even some of his professors and teammates would express such opposition.

The racist attitudes we were up against were monumental. Even one of my top athletic boosters said one day, "You know what? Every time Jerry scores a touchdown he gets whiter and whiter." I can't imagine how things like that made Jerry feel.

The boys at SMU were hungry for victory. They had been in a dry streak so they were willing to listen to me. I called in the individual leaders by position and told them about Jerry and his ability to help us win. I asked for their help with their teammates at each position. Most of our players hadn't played an athletic sport with a black person, and some of their grandparents were still fighting the Civil War. Emotions ran deep, and it was up to me—and the coaching staff—to model proper attitudes.

To this day, I haven't made a lot of things public, because most good people wouldn't even believe the bad things that took place. Law enforcement was continually informing me of threats against us, and they encouraged me to keep things quiet from a public standpoint in order to prevent a lot of sick people from being triggered to do something disastrous. I shared just enough with my assistant coaches to put them on alert.

Jerry knew that my door was always open for him, and after he'd share his frustration, I'd always tell him the same thing: "Levi, if you don't want 'em to get your goat, don't tell 'em where it's hid." I cared too much to let him give up on everything.

My secretary screened all of Jerry's calls and mail, watching for threats. I had to talk with his professors and explain the situation Jerry was facing so that none of it would interfere with his grades. Sleepy Morgan, our freshman coach, took Jerry under his wing, and I think all the coaches and players did accept Jerry eventually. He is such a likable guy.

Jerry was a winner before he ever put on an SMU jersey. He was a Bible-believing Christian and a moral person with an incredible work ethic. All I did was help him to discover what he already had inside, and to introduce the nation to a person of outstanding character and talent.

Many of us will never experience the pain of racism, but all of us face adversity of some sort, and when life knocks us down we have to get up and keep pressing forward. If we allow life to get us down, we're giving adversity too much power.

I would still be coaching if it weren't for cancer, but I have had the opportunity to meet so many good people as I make speeches for the Cancer Foundation, to help raise money for cancer research. Although there's still a long way to go, researchers are making gains. Perhaps one day, if we don't give up, we will have a cure. Either way, we all have a question to answer every day: Will I let adversity beat me, or will I use adversity to make a positive difference?

12

SUCCESS IN SUCCESSION

Leaving a winning legacy

WHAT IS THE American dream, anyway? What creates a winning legacy? Is it money? Power? Success?

Let's start with money. Every year, millions of people buy lottery tickets in search of happiness and every year people like Willie Hurt of Michigan win. But do they really *win?* Just two years after receiving $3.1 million, Willie was flat broke, divorced, and charged with murder. Eight years after Janite Lee of Missouri won $18 million, she filed for bankruptcy and had a grand total of $700 remaining in her bank account. Ken Proxmire quit his job after winning the Michigan lottery, but was back to work as a machinist within five years after filing for bankruptcy. One couple "enjoyed" their $4.2 million lottery win for a whopping eleven years before going broke and getting divorced.[1]

Beyond Xs and Os

Sadly, there are dozens of similar stories, leading some to believe that money only buys happiness when it is earned the old-fashioned way. Let's take a look. There are thousands of wealthy executives on Wall Street today who scraped their way to the top, working unbelievably long hours and sacrificing much of themselves to achieve their financial success. Surely their gigantic bank accounts, yacht excursions, beautiful wives, and millionaire estates deliver the sort of authentic happiness and winning legacy they fought for. Or, maybe not.

In the wake of our most recent financial crisis, a record number of wealthy couples, those with $10 million or more in assets, are filing for divorce. The divorce caseload of one New York law firm increased more than 20 percent within just months of the stock market plummet, their largest single increase in thirty years. One millionaire husband is so convinced that his wife will leave him if she discovers their $12 million loss in net worth that he borrows money to maintain her lifestyle and disguise their true financial condition.[2]

If money doesn't guarantee a winning legacy, then it must be power. Power is invigorating. It has been the basis of superhero stories and blockbuster movies for decades. If you have power, if you have control, then you will also have happiness. Whether an investment firm or a football team, every business in the world has positions of power, and some of the most prominent positions are found in Washington, D.C. I can think of few positions more prestigious than those held by men and women elected by their peers and granted the power to make decisions on our behalf. Unfortunately, many of them forget that their power comes with a great deal of responsibility.

A quick Google search reveals dozens of books about the culture of corruption in D.C. The news of U.S. senators and representatives coming under federal investigation for everything from sex scandals to bribery is all too familiar. Ted Stevens of Alaska was convicted on seven counts of bribery and tax evasion.[3] Tim Mahoney of Florida agreed to pay his former mistress $121,000 while promising his constituents a "world that is safer and more moral."[4] Charles Rangel of New York, head of the congressional committee that writes the country's tax laws, is repeatedly investigated by the House ethics committee for failing to report income.[5] Duke Cunningham of California pleaded guilty to conspiracy to commit bribery, mail and wire fraud, and tax evasion.[6] And we're just getting started. Apparently, power doesn't guarantee a winning legacy either.

That means it must be success. Surely success is the answer. America is the land of opportunity and the land of champions. We have great athletes and great athletic programs. Few things rival the site of a football stadium painted in the colors of its team's uniform, and we all love a great success story about a kid from the inner city making it to the pros. Every kid in America has dreamed of being Michael Jordan or Brett Favre. In fact, more than a few kids dreamed of being Michael Vick.

Vick grew up in impoverished Newport News, Virginia, and football was his ticket out. If he could find success in the game he loved, he believed he would be happy. He received his first football at age three and went on to have a record-breaking football career as a high school quarterback, where he ran and passed for nearly 6,000 yards and 61 touchdowns.[7]

Verna Berthel with her sons

At Virginia Tech, Vick was named the Big East Conference Rookie of the Year in 1999, won the Best College Football Player ESPY Award in 2000, and was named the 2001 Gator Bowl MVP. He was a success. Vick left college early to play for the Atlanta Falcons, where he won the ESPY for Best NFL Player in 2003, was named to Forbes Top 100 Celebrities list in 2005, and earned lucrative sponsorships from companies like Nike, EA Sports, and Coca-Cola. It's no wonder kids wanted to be Michael Vick. He was a success. But was he happy? Had he achieved a winning legacy? Apparently not.

Just two years after the peak of Michael Vick's success, he was sentenced to twenty-three months in federal prison for promoting, funding, and facilitating a "cruel and inhumane" dogfighting operation.[8] Great success in his football career was not enough. Fortunately, Michael Vick appears to have overcome these poor choices. He has served his debt to society and I believe it's a good thing that he is getting a second chance in football and in life.

So, what is it then? If money, power, and success don't deliver authentic happiness and a winning legacy, what is the answer?

There are two people in my life, in addition to Deanna, who consistently show me the answer to achieving the American dream and leaving a winning legacy. One is Hayden and the other is my mom. One makes headlines and has national name recognition, and the other leads a quiet life with little fanfare.

My mom is one of the best examples of a winning legacy I have ever seen. She never went to college. She didn't build a Fortune 500 company or win the Nobel Peace Prize. She isn't rich or famous. I'm pretty sure she never starts her days with the purpose of leaving a winning legacy, but she has done it simply by living right.

If anyone has had a reason to complain or wallow in self-pity, it's my mom, but she is one of the hardest workers I have ever known, and I have rarely heard her complain about pain, inconvenience, or lack of money. She simply gets out of bed every day and does what needs to be done. When raising me and my twelve brothers and sisters, Mom demonstrated love every day and taught us the virtue of caring for others and the importance of minding our manners. She sacrificed her own comfort in order to make us comfortable and always encouraged us to follow our dreams. When Dad was dying of cancer, she worked even harder and gave even more of herself, without complaining.

Beyond Xs and Os

As I look back at the emotional and physical demands she endured during those difficult times, always keeping a positive attitude, I am utterly amazed at her psychological strength. The winning legacy she has given me has nothing to do with money, power, or success, and everything to do with psychology. Very few things in life are under our control. We cannot control the stock market or keep our loved ones from getting sick, but we can control how we respond to life. I've learned that, like Mom, I have the opportunity to leave a positive legacy simply by maintaining a positive attitude, living with integrity, persevering through adversity, and investing in people.

Front Row (L-R): Bill Dervrich, Bill Brashier, Bernie Wyatt, Barry Alvarez, Dan McCarney
Back Row (L-R): Bill Snyder, Del Miller, Carl Jackson, Hayden Fry, Kirk Ferentz, Don Patterson, Bruce Kittle

1985 Hawkeyes coaching staff

I will never forget walking into Hayden's family room several years ago and seeing five big-screen televisions, tuned to five different college football games being coached by five of his previous assistants—Bob Stoops at Oklahoma, Bill Snyder at Kansas State, Barry Alvarez at Wisconsin, Dan McCarney at Iowa State, and Kirk Ferentz—carrying on Hayden's tradition at Iowa. What a feeling. Hayden isn't a sappy guy, but he watched those games like a proud father. He had more than twenty coaching assistants who went on to become college or professional coaches; twenty-six players who became assistant coaches; and several players who went on to the NFL. Though it is nearly impossible to track Hayden's entire sphere of influence, it is impossible to ignore his legacy.

In fact, I hope that every page of this book is a tribute to Hayden's winning legacy—not the number of football games he won, but to the impact he has had on the world of football and still has in the lives of others. His friendship has taught me so much about living right, and it motivates me every day to persevere, grow, and get better in my personal life and my business life.

Whether inspiring belief in others or cultivating a productive culture, Hayden knows that attitude is everything. If you don't believe you can win, you won't. If you don't have an attitude of personal responsibility, you won't be responsible. If you don't have an attitude of togetherness, you will never be a team.

Hayden leads by example, with uncompromising character. When everyone in the Southwest Conference believed in recruiting only white football players, Hayden took a stand for what was right and recruited Jerry LeVias. In a world that

Hayden and Tom

idolizes sports icons, Hayden refuses to take himself or his success too seriously. He learned from H. L. Hunt that no level of success warrants getting too big for one's britches. Integrity is the compass Hayden used to navigate a legendary career and impact generations to come.

It is Hayden's commitment to invest in people that causes his legacy to multiply. If his players were having a bad practice, he called them together for a sing-along. When they arrived in the fall, prepared for conditioning drills, he had them just talk to each other instead. If one of his players had a dog named Spot, he knew all about Spot. He looked past the stats, and evaluated each player and coach as a whole person. As you know by now, Hayden loves to win, but he never compromised himself or others to do so.

Perhaps this is why his legacy lives on in people like Barry Alvarez. Alvarez was one of Hayden's assistants at Iowa in the early 1980s and went on to become Wisconsin's all-time winningest coach. In his sixteen seasons at Wisconsin, he became known for his uncompromising values and never giving up on his blueprint for the program's success.[9] Sound familiar?

Another of Hayden's assistants, Bob Stoops (or "Bobby," as Hayden calls him), is in the process of growing his own impressive legacy as the head coach at the University of Oklahoma. A two-time national coach of the year, Stoops refuses to win at the expense of integrity. He once dismissed one of his most promising freshmen after the player posted a vulgar rap video of himself on the Internet. One sportswriter pays homage to Stoops by writing that his actions make it "obvious that winning with integrity can be done."[10] Sound familiar?

Coach Fry with Barry Alvarez

Kirk Ferentz, Hayden's offensive line coach at Iowa from 1981 to 1989, went on to coach in the NFL before returning to Iowa as head coach when Hayden retired. Ferentz is known for building solid foundations rather than making quick fixes, and says his team is "not backing down from anyone. And we're having fun." He also claims that one of the best things about his job as head coach is that he can't blame anyone but himself when things get screwed up.[11] Sound familiar?

During Hayden's last year at Iowa and just before playing their rival, Iowa State, he warned his coaching staff not to underestimate the Cyclones, reminding them that "The sun don't shine on the same dog's rump every day." The head coach of Iowa State at the time happened to be Dan McCarney, who had served as one of Hayden's assistant coaches at Iowa for more than a decade. At the end of the day, McCarney led Iowa State to a 27–9 victory and broke the Hawkeyes' fifteen-game winning streak against his Cyclones.

Under the circumstances, the game must have been bittersweet for both men, and McCarney told reporters that meeting Hayden at midfield following the game was one of the most heartwarming postgame exchanges he had ever experienced. Hayden complimented McCarney's players and staff and expressed sincere affection for his former assistant. "You can't imagine how much that meant to me," McCarney said. "The man's meant everything to me."[12]

Hayden loves to win, but he cares way more about developing winning people, and he never sacrifices people for wins. Building a lasting legacy is not quick; it happens over time with a great deal of perseverance and a commitment to living right.

My grandfather lost his farm to the Great Depression, despite a lifetime of hard work and dedication. I've often tried to comprehend the pain and fear he must have felt, but there is no way I ever will. One of the things he learned, and would say frequently, is that people have to build a solid foundation within their life's work, because "you can only eat so much, drink so much, and sleep so much."

I don't care how much money you have, how much power you have, or how much success you have—it isn't enough. The only thing that provides authentic happiness is living a meaningful life and investing in people. I feel unbelievably blessed to have discovered the true essence of the American dream; it's not about dollars, but about the intangibles. By empowering those around

Hayden Fry and Tom's mother, Verna Berthel

me, living with integrity, and valuing relationships, I am assured that my life is not being lived in vain. I don't want my life to die with me.

Just as my mom and Hayden have written their legacies on my life, I hope that I am writing a positive legacy on the lives of others. Hayden and I both love to win. Still, we have both learned that leaving a winning legacy is much more about how you play the game than what the score is when the clock runs out.

POSTGAME WITH COACH FRY

Success in succession

It's impossible to mention every person who made a difference in my life as a result of my football career; the list includes fellow coaches, opposing coaches, players, entertainers . . . even administrators. I have been incredibly fortunate to associate with some real quality people, and I hesitate to mention names for fear of leaving someone out. Still, there are some stories that come to mind.

Take Bill Snyder, for instance. Bill and I worked together for a couple of years at North Texas before we both made the move to Iowa, where he led the Hawkeye offense for ten years. He is such a focused and determined guy, and probably the most demanding coach on technique I ever had. I remember running some passing drills with Chuck

Long throwing the ball. Every time Chuck threw the ball, even if it was a completion, Bill had a correction. "Chuck, you over-strided," he'd say. Or "You didn't turn your thumb down, Chuck. You gotta remember to turn your thumb down when you throw the ball."

After several throws, and several corrections, I walked over to Bill and said, "Coach Snyder, just let the kid throw the ball one time without you correcting him." I could immediately see the blood vessels pop up in his neck and his face begin to turn red. That was it. I never corrected Bill again after that. He is truly a perfectionist, and it showed in the great offense he put together at Iowa. Later on, when Bill accepted the

Chuck Long

Photo Credit: UIowa Photo Service

head-coaching position at Kansas State, he did one of the finest jobs ever of turning a football program around.

It was likely Bill's influence that made Chuck Long such a standout player. I've never seen a cooler, more unflappable quarterback than Chuck. Regardless of what happened in a game, how hard he got hit or how many turnovers there were, Chuck never lost his cool. Well, except for once. It was his freshman year and he had started the game against Nebraska. They were pounding us 28–0 before halftime, and I just wanted to get the last play off and get to the locker room so we could make some corrections. I told Chuck what play to run. He hustled to the line of scrimmage, got under center, and almost immediately called time-out. That didn't go over too well with me. *What in blazes is he doing?* I thought to myself as I motioned for him to come to the sideline. Well, he ran over, looking a little pale, stopped about three feet from me, and threw up all over the bottom of my white pants and shoes. That's the only time I ever saw Chuck shook up.

Fortunately, I had a clean change of clothes in the locker room. Bless his heart, he apologized and went back out and ran the play just fine. Chuck was runner-up to Bo Jackson for the Heisman Trophy his senior year in the closest Heisman Trophy race ever. I'm really proud of all Chuck accomplished. He went on to become a collegiate head coach at San Diego State and is currently the offensive coordinator at Kansas.

Dan McCarney is another guy who left his impression on me. We had a great relationship both on and off the field, and I don't mind saying that I was not happy when Iowa State let him go. He took the Cyclones to a bowl game five out of his last six years, and that's just incredible. He is an exceptional coach and a fine gentleman. I'll never forget losing to him

Kirk Ferentz

during my last year with the Hawkeyes. I hate to lose, but I was so proud of Dan and so happy for him. He has a bright career ahead.

When I came to Iowa, one of the guys I inherited was Bobby Stoops. What an outstanding leader and bright young man. He really knows football. Of course, he had a great teacher in his father, who was a very successful high school coach in Ohio, and who very effectively passed on his work ethic and football knowledge to his boys. For years, Bobby has been doing the same thing with dozens of young players. I just couldn't be more proud of what Bobby has accomplished.

When I had to step away from coaching, and Iowa was struggling to decide whether Bobby or Kirk (Ferentz) would replace me, it was going right down to the wire. Bobby called me from Atlanta after having interviewed for the head-coaching position with Oklahoma and receiving a job offer. Iowa hadn't made a decision yet, and Bobby called to ask my advice. He didn't have much time to make the decision. I told him, "Son, you've got a bird in the hand and Oklahoma is a heck of a school." He is like a son to me, and though I would have loved to see him at Iowa, I didn't want to see him pass up a sure opportunity that would be a positive move for him. With eleven consecutive winning seasons, eleven bowl appearances, and a growing legacy of assistants who are head coaches in other Division 1-A programs, I'd say it's worked out pretty well for him.

Obviously, Kirk Ferentz did get the Iowa offer and has proven to be a super recruiter and a prince of a guy. He's a great coach and an even better friend. Just look at how many players he has coached to be better young men and to live and play with a high degree of integrity and commitment. Kirk has been named Big Ten Coach of the Year a three times (2002, 2004, and 2009), and his assistants have received their share of national recognition as well. To date, five of his players have been national Players of the Year at their position and nearly seventy of his senior starters have gone on to sign with NFL teams. Most important, Iowa is tied for the highest graduation rate in the nation among top-rated college football programs. Kirk is in the ideal spot and he has a lot of success still ahead. Watching the success of my guys is way more rewarding to me than anything I ever achieved personally.

Barry Alvarez is another guy that's been fun to watch. I had become good friends with Bob Devaney at Nebraska, and later, Tom Osborne, so I was asked to speak at their football clinics when Barry was a linebacker for them. After college, Barry coached high school football in Lexington, Nebraska, and then in Mason City, where his team won the state championship and six of his players from the championship team went on to play at Division I schools. When I came to the University of Iowa, I needed to hire a couple of guys from Iowa to help us recruit. They had to be highly successful and respected—guys the high school coaches would listen to.

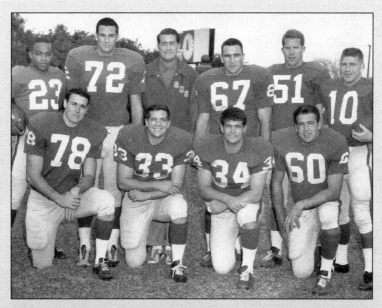

1966 SMU Mustangs, with Jerry LeVias and Coach Fry in the back row

Barry fit the bill perfectly and he did a great job for us before going on to Notre Dame.

He called me one time and asked what I thought about him interviewing at Wisconsin. "Barry," I said, "Wisconsin is a sleeping giant. They just need leadership. They've got the personnel and the kids are real smart coming out of high school up there. They're big, physical kids." Well, he took the job and ended up reviving that program beautifully. He became the all-time winningest coach in the history of Wisconsin football, and he led them to three Big Ten championships and three Rose Bowl games. In 1997, after a long winning streak over Wisconsin, we came up short. Barry was coaching and once again, I couldn't help but be so proud of him and what he'd accomplished.

I've already talked about the Jerry LeVias days, but I'll mention him again here because there's another story that comes to mind. Levi is one of the best public speakers I've ever heard, and he's got a great sense of humor. He and I recently appeared in a documentary for HBO about the integration of college football, and one of our best interview moments never made it into the final show. At the end of one of our interviews the moderator asked me very directly what I really thought about Jerry. I sort of straightened up, very pleased to answer his question, and said, "Well, he's just like a son to me."

Jerry started laughing and said, "Coach, if you're going to be my daddy, you better start working on your suntan." It's that sort of attitude and sense of humor that got us both through some real difficult days.

I could go on for pages about the guys I've coached with and the players I've coached. Bo Pelini, Dave Tripplett, Mike Stoops, John Austin, Donny Patterson, Jim Levitt, Bum Philips, Andy Everest, Bobby Diaco, Frank Verducci, Jerry Montgomery, Glenn Gossett, Pug Gabriel, Larry Horton, John O'Hara, Bernie Wyatt, Dave Smith, Ray Utley, Dudley Parker, Jerry Moore, Jonathan Hayes, Bobby Elliot, Billy Inge, Mark Hendrickson, Sleepy Morgan, Al Everest, Herb Zimmerman, Tom Brown, Chuck Curtis, Charlie Driver, Clovis Hale, Howard Cissell, Brett Bielema, Del Miller, Carl Jackson, Ed Crowley, Paul Longo, Eddy Lane, John Strief . . . I could go on and

Tom and Hayden

on. Coach Bill Brashier was with me for twenty-three years and turned down head-coaching jobs. He loved his job as defensive coordinator.

Each one of these guys has a special place in my heart. To see each of them grow as individuals and perform with such success is a great thrill, and each one is a powerful reminder of how much the good Lord has blessed me. I'm so grateful.

In the pages of this book, Tom Berthel captures the essence of what I've tried to stand for over the years. I'm so appreciative to him for that, and it's not because I've done anything all that great. It's because the people I've had with me are great. Every person in our lives has something to teach us, if we'll just be quiet and listen. We might learn what not to do at times, but we're still learning. A legacy isn't something a person can muster up on a Saturday afternoon. It's something that grows slowly, day by day, year by year, through blood, sweat, and tears. It's not something we can force, but something that simply happens while people watch us go about our business. Make no mistake about it, as tough as it might be at times: Life is a game worth playing. Play it to win and enjoy every single step of the journey.

NOTES

CHAPTER 5: Modeling the Way

1. Delano, D. (2001). "The economy seems likely to dodge a recession." *Modern Materials Handling.* Retrieved August 27, 2008, from www.mmh.com/article/CA154335.html.
2. Boshart, R. (2008). "Iowa flood losses hard to fathom." GazetteOnline.com. Retrieved August 27, 2008, from www.gazetteonline.com/apps/pbcs.dll/article?AID=/20080815/NEWS/27792448/1006/news.

CHAPTER 6: The Psychology of Team

1. *U-571.* Dir. Jonathan Mostow. Universal Studios Home Entertainment, 2000.

CHAPTER 7: Know Where You Are on the Field

1. BookRags Staff. (2005). "Encyclopedia of World Biography on H. L. Hunt." BookRags.com. Retrieved September 24, 2008, from www.bookrags.com/biography/h-l-hunt.

CHAPTER 8: The Art of Anticipation

1. Metelko, K. (2002). "Titanic's maiden voyage." Retrieved October 15, 2008 from: www.webtitanic.net.

2. RMS Titanic, Inc. (1987–2010). "Turkish, electric, and swimming baths." Retrieved May 13, 2010 from: http://www.titanic-online.com/index.php4?page=94.

3. *Titanic's lifeboats.* Retrieved October 15, 2008 from: http://www.titanic-titanic.com/lifeboats.shtml.

4. Titanic Research & Modeling Association. (2005) "Tech feature of the month: Titanic's double bottom." Retrieved October 16, 2008 from: http://titanic-model.com/articles/tech/TechFeature June2005.htm.

5. Ostrowski, J. (2001). "The unsinkable RMS Titanic." Retrieved October 15, 2008 from: www.titanicstory.com.

6. *Titanic's lifeboats.* Retrieved October 15, 2008 from: http://www.titanic-titanic.com/lifeboats.shtml.

7. Ostrowski, J. (2001). "The unsinkable RMS Titanic." Retrieved October 15, 2008 from: www.titanicstory.com.

8. *The Guardian:* "The Titanic is sunk, with great loss of life." Tuesday, April 16 1912: p.34: http://www.guardian.co.uk/news/1912/apr/16/leadersandreply.mainsection.

9. *The New York Times:* April 27, 1912: "Saw rockets as Titanic sank, captain admits." Retrieved October 16, 2008: http://query.nytimes.com/gst/abstract.html?res=94 03E3DE153CE633A25754C2A9629C946396D6CF.

10. Gracie, A. (2004). *The truth about the Titanic.* Whitefish, MT: Kessinger Publishing.

11. Chambers, K. (2000). *Icebergs.* Retrieved October 15, 2008 from: http://www.weather.com/newscenter/atmospheres/feature/110100feature.html.

CHAPTER 9: Diversification

1. Zarroli, J. (2007). "Black Monday: A bad day led to many changes." NPR.org. Retrieved December 27, 2008, from www.npr.org/templates/story/story.php?storyId=15436586.

2. Brouwer, K. (2008). "Key Rates: 1980 vs. 2008." Fundmastery Blog. Retrieved on December 27, 2008, from www.fundmasteryblog.com/2008/11/26/key-rates-1980-vs-2008.

3. Sungard. (2002). "U.S. savings and loan crisis." ERisk. Retrieved on December 26, 2008, from www.erisk.com/Learning/CaseStudies/USSavingsLoanCrisis.asp.

CHAPTER 10: Uncompromising Character

1. Fox Business News. (2008). "AIG executives blow $440,000 after getting bailout." Retrieved November 12, 2008, from www.foxbusiness.com/story/markets/industries/finance/aig-executives-blow--getting-bailout/.

2. *The Wall Street Journal.* (2005). "AIG reports' integrity questioned." Retrieved November 12, 2008, from http://money.cnn.com/2005/04/26/news/fortune500/aig.dj/index.htm.

3. *The Straits Times.* (2008). "Bailed-out AIG denies excesses for staff." Retrieved November 12, 2008, from www.straitstimes.com/Breaking%2BNews/Money/Story/STIStory_301353.html.

4. White, Paul. (2007). "What is a 'good work ethic,' really?" Dr. Paul White, Licensed Psychologist. Retrieved November 12, 2008, from http://drpaulwhite.com/blog/2007/03/19/what-is-a-good-work-ethic-really/.

5. Articles Referenced: "Five football players suspended for involvement in on-campus fight" (www.orlandosentinel.com); "Football player arrested in stabbing near campus" (www.statejournal.com); "College president arrested for DUI" (www.wzzm13.com); "High teacher arrested on drug charges" (www.chron.com); "Human resources chief faces embezzlement charge" (www.northcountrygazette.org); and "Sheriff indicted on federal conspiracy charges" (http://ap.google.com).

CHAPTER 11: Adversity as Opportunity

1. Manning, J. (2000). "The Midwest farm crisis of the 1980s." The Eighties Club: The Politics and Pop Culture of the 1980s. Retrieved from http://eightiesclub.tripod.com/id395.htm.
2. Hamilton, A. (1998). "Fry touched state, farmers, players." *The Daily Iowan,* Iowa City.
3. Ecker, J. (1993). "NCAA says NO to ANF." *The Gazette,* Iowa City and Cedar Rapids.
4. Chavez, A. (2007). "Former SMU football player recounts trials of integration." *TCU Daily Skiff,* Fort Worth. Retrieved from www.tcudailyskiff.com.
5. Sports Editors. (2009). *Inside Slant.* Southern Methodist Team Report. Fox Sports. http://msn.foxsports.com/cfb/team/southern-methodist-mustangs-football/teamreport
6. "Jerry LeVias: A marked man." (2003) Business Wire: Dallas. Retrieved from http://findarticles.com/p/articles/mi_m0EIN/is_2003_Dec_2/ai_110744214/.

CHAPTER 12: Success in Succession

1. Goodstein, E. (2006). "Unlucky lottery winners who lost their money." Bankrate.com. Retrieved January 6, 2009, from www.bankrate.com/msn/news/advice/2004 1108a1.asp.

2. Bawden, T. (2008). "Credit crunch raises divorce rate for America's superwealthy." Times Online. Retrieved January 6, 2009, from http://women.timesonline.co.uk/tol/life_ and_style/women/relationships/article4312508.ece.

3. Johnson, C. and Kane, P. (2008). "Sen. Stevens indicted on 7 corruption counts." *The Washington Post.* Retrieved January 6, 2009 from: http://www.washingtonpost.com/ wp-dyn/content/article/2008/07/29/AR2008072901416. html?nav=hcmodule.

4. Schwartz, E. (2008). "Congressman's $121,000 payoff to alleged mistress." ABC News. Retrieved January 6, 2009, from http://abcnews.go.com/Blotter/Politics/ Story?id=5997043&page=1.

5. Dealey, S. (2008). "Another Rangel property scandal?" *U.S. News & World Report.* Retrieved January 6, 2009, from: www.usnews.com/blogs/sam-dealey/2008/09/05/ another-rangel-property-scandal.html.

6. Henry, E. and Preston, M. (2005). "Congressman resigns after bribery plea." CNN.com. Retrieved January 6, 2009, from www.cnn.com/2005/POLITICS/11/28/ cunningham/.

7. Michael Vick biography. JockBio.com. Retrieved January 6, 2009, from www.jockbio.com/Bios/Vick/Vick_bio.html.

8. Associated Press. (2007). "Michael Vick sentenced to 23 months in jail for role in dogfighting conspiracy." Fox News. Retrieved January 6, 2009, from www.foxnews.com/story/0,2933,316319,00.html.

9. Amazon Editorial Review. *Don't Flinch—Barry Alvarez: The Autobiography.* Retrieved from www.amazon.com/Dont-Flinch-Autobiography-Wisconsins-Winningest/dp/097587697X.

10. Hillman, J. (2008). "Stoops makes right decision." RealFootball365.com. Retrieved January 10, 2009, from www.realfootball365.com/articles/oklahoma/12272#author.

11. Blaudschun, M. (2005). "Heavenly state for Iowa." Boston.com. Retrieved January 10, 2009, from www.boston.com/sports/colleges/football/articles/2005/09/01/heavenly_state_for_iowa/.

12. Peterson, R. (2004). "Hayden Fry, University of Iowa, 2004." *Des Moines Register.* Retrieved January 10, 2009, from www.desmoinesregister.com/apps/pbcs.dll/article?AID=/20040704/SPORTS11/50708005.

ACKNOWLEDGMENTS

WHILE TRAVELING MANY miles on planes in the early days of building our company, trying to maintain a balance between work and my family life, I began to get the idea that I would like to write this book about all of the inspiration that Hayden has given to me. While Hayden is the center of this story, I owe a debt of gratitude to many people for assisting me with completing the dream of writing my first book as well as for enriching my life.

First, to my wife Deanna and our children, Paige and Brandon, for always providing me with encouragement and motivation.

My family at Berthel Fisher, reps and employees alike, particularly Ron Brendengen, for always being one of my "head coaches." Dwight Wheelan, Fred Fisher, Julie Driscoll, and others who helped with this book, and in building our company. To Shelli Brady for photo assistance, and Mandy and Lynn for their willingness to be there when I needed them.

I'd like to show my appreciation to my mother and the other members of my family. Also, thanks to Tom and Jane Saxen and Jim Arenson who encouraged me to keep the book moving along. Thanks to Bob Vander Plaats, and to Carl Johnson, who introduced us, and Kristi Dusenberry, who so believed in the project and did a tremendous job bringing it to life.

Thanks to Skyhorse Publishing and to Mark Weinstein for seeing the potential in *Beyond Xs and Os*, and for your dedication in facilitating the project to completion. A special thank you to the Roeder family for providing some amazing photos from Ted's collection (what a tribute to his memory), and to Max Conde for assisting in endorsements.

I would especially like to thank Shirley Fry, who inspired and assisted me when and where it was needed. Kirk Ferentz for not only honoring Hayden and me, but for inspiring readers by authoring the foreword and continuing the success and tradition of Iowa Football. Bob Stoops for endorsing the book.

Finally I'd like to thank the University of Iowa for introducing me to Hayden and Coach Fry, for continuing to give me the inspiration to go for it!

ABOUT THE AUTHOR

Thomas J. Berthel is chief executive officer, president, and chairman of the board of Berthel Fisher & Company, a financial services holding firm located in Marion, Iowa. Since founding the company  in 1985, Tom has led his team through the trials, tribulations, and accomplishments that have accompanied twenty-five years' worth of market changes. Representing nearly 400 registered representatives in 41 states, a subsidiary of Berthel Fisher is ranked among the top fifty independent broker/dealers in the industry.

Prior to establishing Berthel Fisher & Company, Tom received his BA in music from St. Ambrose College in Davenport, Iowa (where he currently serves on the board). He later earned his MBA from the University of Iowa, where his mentor, legend Hayden Fry, spent many years as head coach.

Not only is Tom committed to his company and his employees, but he is also dedicated to sharing his knowledge and good fortune with several charitable organizations including The American Cancer Society and the Variety Club of Eastern Iowa.

While Tom is no stranger to inspirational speeches, articles, and presentations, this is his first penned narrative. With this book he hopes to share some of Coach Fry's inspiration with his own teammates, as well as other business leaders nationwide, sports fans and many others.

Tom and wife Deanna Berthel have two adult children and two grandchildren. Outside the office, he is passionately involved in the political process and spends his downtime enjoying the game of golf.

POST GAME

Hayden Fry spent thirty-eight years behind the whistle as a head football coach, taking on the challenge of elevating losing programs into winners. He coached at Southern Methodist University, the University of North Texas, and the University of Iowa. During his twenty years at Iowa, he won three Big Ten Championships. He was named Coach of the Year multiple times in the Big Ten Conference, the Southwest Conference, and the Missouri Valley Conference, and was selected ABC National Coach of the Year in 1982.

Hayden was a captain in the U.S. Marine Corps and also was a quarterback on the 1953 USMC football championship team. In 1954 he was the quarterback on the All Far East Service Championship Team in Japan. Other accomplishments include awarding the first African-American College Scholarship in the Southwest Conference in 1964; serving as president of the American Football Coaches Association in 1993; having sixteen teams participate in bowl games; being inducted into the College Football Hall of Fame in 2003; and being awarded the Amos Alonzo Stagg Award in 2005 for recognition of outstanding service in the advancement of the best interests of football. Seventeen of Coach Fry's former assistants have gone on to become head coaches in college or NFL programs.

INDEX

MORE BOOKS FOR THE COLLEGE FOOTBALL LOVER

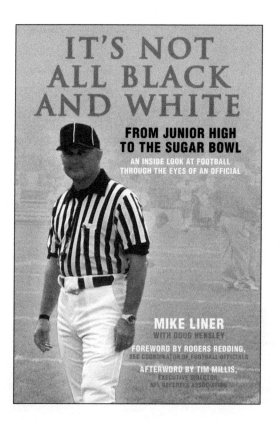

It's Not All Black and White
From Junior High to the Sugar Bowl, an Inside Look at Football Through the Eyes of an Official
by Mike Liner with Doug Hensley
Foreword by Rogers Redding, SEC Coordinator of Football Officials
Afterword by Tim Millis, Executive Director, NFL Referees Association

From junior high football games to the Sugar Bowl with a national championship up for grabs, Mike Liner has seen it all in football. President and CEO of a bank by day, Liner has been a Texas football official on Fridays and Saturdays for the past thirty-five years. *It's Not All Black and White* offers a view of college football seen through a different set of eyes: the eyes of an official. Liner takes readers through the story of his ascension up the officiating hierarchy and describes the bumps in the road he encountered along the way. In doing so, he puts a human face on an aspect of football that all too often is dehumanized—the officiating of the game.

With a foreword by the SEC Coordinator of Football Officials, Rogers Redding, and an afterword by Tim Millis, Executive Director, NFL Referees Association, *It's Not All Black and White* lifts the curtain on big-time college football, revealing what Liner saw as he observed it and why the game means so much to him. Liner also recounts important lessons he learned through football about life as a business leader, as a family man, and as someone whose faith has grown through the years.

$22.95 Hardcover • 256 pages

MORE BOOKS FOR THE COLLEGE FOOTBALL LOVER

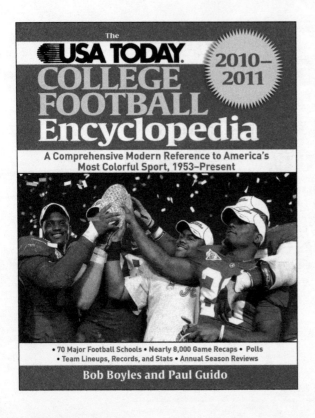

"If you are a real student of college football, this book is for you. There are so many facts crammed into it that only my offensive linemen could lift it!"

—Joe Gibbs, former Head Coach, Washington Redskins

The USA TODAY 2010–2011 College Football Encyclopedia
A Comprehensive Modern Reference to America's Most Colorful Sport, 1953–Present
by Bob Boyles and Paul Guido

The result of fifteen years of exhaustive research, *The USA TODAY 2010–2011 College Football Encyclopedia* is without question the most comprehensive resource on college football ever set to type. Authors Bob Boyles and Paul Guido love college football with a passion and undertook to pore through more than 4,000 media guides, watch thousands of hours of game films, and read through just about every book ever published on the game to bring this massive reference to fruition. In these pages you will find information unavailable in any other single publication:

- Recaps of nearly 8,000 games
- Detailed reviews of more than 57 college football seasons
- Complete season-by-season lineups and records of more than 70 major programs
- Personality profiles of some of the game's biggest stars and coaches
- Season-by-season award winners, all-American teams, polls, and NFL drafts
- And much more!

With 1,400 pages of facts, figures, and history, this is the ultimate book for the fan, fully updated for the new college football season!

$24.95 Paperback • 1,400 pages